They Lived Happily Ever After

Methods for achieving happy
endings in coupling.

by

Leslie Cameron Bandler

Meta Publications
Cupertino, California 95014
1978

DEDICATION

I dedicate this book with great affection
  To my brother Wade
    May you live happily ever after
    and
  To my parents Harry and Joyce
    For teaching me to stand on my own feet instead of someone
    elses toes.

ACKNOWLEDGMENTS

For patience and support given far above and beyond any call of duty. I would like to thank my husband, Richard, my son Mark, and my dear friend Adrienne.

TABLE OF CONTENTS

FORWARD

Since the beginning of time itself, mystery has always existed.
Since the beginning of civilization itself three types of geniuses
have always existed. The first type consists of people who have the
unique quality of being able to identify a mystery. These thinkers
have always demonstrated the power of searching through the
obvious to locate the unknown. Newton and Freud were such
people. The second type of genius consists of people who could,
through whatever mechanism, unravel mystery and harness the
tremendous resources that were always potentially available.
These thinkers and doers have always demonstrated the usefulness
of tenacity and are themselves the main staple of progress in all
academic disciplines. Such people include Linus Pauling, Madame
Curie and many others. The third type of genius is those few
individuals who have the ability to take esoteric knowledge and
make it useful, comprehensible, and available to a large number of
people. The discovery of electricity is only valuable in that we have
Thomas Edisons who can make it both useful and accessible to the
people of the world. Knowledge in a vacuum is still part of a
vacuum. Give it form and substance, and its meaning will have a
pervasive impact on human kind.

The author of this book, Leslie Cameron Bandler, possesses
some of each of these three qualities. My mind has been expanded
by her ability to identify mystery, my thoughts have been clarified
into harmony by her ability to unravel mystery, and my world has
been expanded by her ability to make those mysteries a phenomenon that can be harnessed by any who have the desire. I have
devoted a substantial portion of the last few years to unraveling the
mysteries of human communication. I believe I have been somewhat successful at harnessing the power and the resources that
come with explicit understanding. During this time Leslie has ex-

plored and extracted patterns of communications with me. Having patterns of communication be explicit, means that they are therefore learnable. That is to say that whatever power and resources we have learned to harness can be harnessed by others willing to learn the mechanisms we use. This however, says nothing about the ease or accessibility of what is needed to be known and done in order to have the benefits of what we have discovered. So it is with great pleasure that I write this introduction because here is another example of Leslie, someone who is very dear to me, demonstrating the degree to which she possesses that third type of genius. Once again she amazes me with her talent at making the complex simple, the esoteric pervasive, and the inaccessible available. This book offers anyone interested in having more of an impact as a communicator, a therapist, or wizard, the opportunity to find a clearly defined path through the overgrown mazes that constitute the structure of magic. It is with the greatest of respect, the deepest of love, and a huge sigh of relief that I say to you

Read on and learn.

Richard Bandler
July 18, 1978

Part I

Preliminaries

Preface

Once upon a time in the not so mythical land of Nom, two very
nice people fell in love. They decided to marry to capture the good
feelings they had for the rest of their natural lives. They thought
love could conquer all and they both fantasized a future of continued joy and growing happiness. As time passed, however, some
mysterious evil lurked furtively around the edge of their joy, and
slowly unseen, unheard and unheralded in any way it began to
work its way into the core of their relationship. Each assumed it
was just a passing mood of the other. As time passed, however,
each began to become more suspect that the other was in some way
bewitched. As time passed even further, every day became more
of a struggle to keep any semblance of the joy that had once
flourished abundantly. Until, it was obvious to each of both of
them that even pretending that things were fine was the utmost of
a chore. Finally, they began accusing each other of being the basis
of the evil, each espousing his own innocence. They sought allies
in their friends and relatives, sides were chosen and open hostilities broke out. The escalation of hostilities continued until finally
"expert" consultants were brought in. Three of the consultants
insisted the problem most definitely was the man's fault, but three
other consultants insisted the problem was most definitely the
woman's fault. Each side expounded elaborate data and theories
to support its claim; the result was further escalation. The man and
the woman could no longer look at each other without feeling
empty, or angry or sometimes great guilt. They would each ask
themselves in moments of solitude "Is it really my fault?" or "How
could they see I'm not to blame?" Time passed even further on

until the whole thing was brought before a legal court to determine the reality of the matter.

A wise and shrewd judge presided over the matter. Charges and counter charges were made. After a time he leaned forward over the bench and said, "Before we proceed any further with this case there is something I must tell you. If one of you is found guilty, you will most certainly be sentenced to a life of complete and utter unhappiness, you will be tortured constantly with excruciating guilt. The other of you will be free to try to find a life of happiness again. It has been my experience through the years that the odds are against you, though it is not impossible. I will offer you a choice. If you are sure beyond a doubt that you are indeed the one who is right I will hear this case and make my decision, however I am not perfect and my decision may be in error. So each of you will risk your future on my fallibility and the strength of your claim. Or you may elect instead to seek the help of a court appointed experience technologist who will provide you with alternatives to knowing the nature of who is indeed right."

This proposal was both frightening and intriguing to the man and the woman, because on the inside neither was sure who was indeed in the right, and everyone had heard of the great powers and mysteries of the experience technologists. So after great discussion and against the advice of their attorneys and consultants, friends and relatives, each decided to face the unknown of an experience technologist rather than risk their future to the whims of a court proceeding.

The next morning both arrived at the laboratory and waited anxiously in the office of the technocrat supervisor. Finally, a man in a white lab jacket entered and silently signaled them to follow him. They passed down corridors lined with rooms that appeared to be filled with huge machines and scientific paraphernalia until they entered a small room darkened except for a red iridescent glow. Three chairs sat in what appeared to be an otherwise empty room. The attendant in the white coat left as the man and the woman sat down and nervously glanced about. Time stood still.

The door of the little room opened and a figure passed in. It was difficult to tell whether it was a man or a woman. The red iridescence reflected off a white lab jacket and produced an eerie glow. Both the man and woman noticed that it seemed to radiate from everywhere and nowhere at the same time. The figure introduced itself as technician 4. The voice still gave no indication of the sex. Technician 4 waved a hand in the air and a small computer terminal emerged from the floor, deft fingers played on the typewriter like keyboard and words emerged on the monitor.

4 turned to each of them and said, "Do you know why you are here?" The man and the woman merely shrugged. "Then let me explain as briefly as I can. You are people who through whatever mechanism have chosen not to find out what went wrong and who was at fault but instead to create a future which is satisfying in itself, thereby relieving the need to know what went wrong. My file here states the problem is a common one. Once there was great love between you but now it is gone. Let me begin by asking you a simple but complex question—Where does love go when it goes away? If there is an answer to this question therein lies the direction to create that satisfying future." Technician 4 paused at this time and looked from the man to the woman, who both being quite confused by all this could only shrug again. The technician continued, "We here at the Institute of Generative Experience offer a variety of futures to people who have your problem. I would like to outline each briefly so you two may come to an agreement about which one you would like.

Technician 4 then reached over to the computer console, deft fingers once again wove an intricate pattern across the keyboard. The red iridescence in the room seemed to shiver for a moment. Then it began to coalesce into an image of a pyramid so that a red translucent pyramid was suspended in the air in the center of the room. The rest of the room was now dark.

Technician 4 began to speak, "I want each of you now to think of one of the pleasant memories from your past, one which is representative of the type of joy you wish to have now." The man and the woman watched the hologram. Suddenly each could see the memory appear in the pyramid. Two people living out events just the way they remembered them, each saw their own memory and each felt sadness that the joy that once was there was no more. The technician continued, "To each of you has appeared an event, if you were to stand and enter the pyramid you would not only see the event from start to finish but also you would hear and feel, smell and taste all that occurred in that time and place. You may try it if you like." The man and the woman stepped into the pyramid. For a moment they only glowed in the iridescent light, then they were both lifted up and transformed into being in the memory; first the man's memory then the woman's. Each memory was joyous and satisfying to both. The technician pressed out the sequence "b-r-e-a-k" return."

The man and the woman stood together in the room now filled with red iridescence. The pyramid was gone but each stared at the other the way they had when love was ever with them. Both sighed deeply and returned to their chairs.

The technician began to speak, "That first program consists of equipping your home with as many of these pyramids as you both can agree you want. Each pyramid holds three events of approximately 6 hours in length. They are quite expensive so you may choose to purchase some now and some at a later date." The man and the woman looked at each other with intense interest. The technician continued, "However I must warn you that most of our past customers have had one or two problems. Either they became bored with reliving the past over and over and purchased a multitude of pyramids until they ran out of pleasant memories or money. Worse yet some stayed in a memory pyramid so long that we were unable to get them out." The technician paused and looked at the man and the woman. "Yet," 4 continued, "With judicious use the memory pyramid offers an alternative to unpleasantness. The second program we offer," the technician reached again to the computer keyboard the iridescence in the room began to shiver once again, coalescing this time into a figure of a brain suspended where the pyramid had been before. The technician continued, "is somewhat simpler and somewhat cheaper, however its much more permanent in nature. The brain you see before you is not a real brain but a blank hologram that can be filled with any thought or belief we choose to put in it. It in essence is nothing more than an elaborate memory bank which can be used to store both data and programs to run that data, or more simply put, we can fill it with facts and belief systems to process those facts." The technician reached again to the computer keyboard punching out a sequence, then stopping and looking intently at the man and the woman. "The second program offers you the following possibility; each of you will believe beyond a doubt that the other is at fault, you will have the total illusion that the other of you has accepted this to be the total truth of the matter. You need only to step into the hologram to try it. We can, of course make this permanent."

The technician paused and gestured to the image of the brain. The woman rose and walked into the image of the brain for a moment. She recalled events which never really transpired and she knew beyond a doubt that she was the one who was wronged and maliciously so. She felt complete righteousness but it did not fill the emptiness inside her. The man followed her and had the same experience.

The technician continued "The drawbacks of this are, of course, that it is imperative that the two of you never meet again. The other drawbacks are self evident. Yet still this is a choice most people consider."

Technician 4 once again let deft fingers weave an intricate pattern of meanings across the computer keyboard. The brain disappeared leaving only the red iridescence in the room. The technician turned to the man and the woman and began to speak, "The third choice we offer you here is a very popular one. This choice offers you a future together, a future of new experience without the risk of unpleasant feelings." The technician turned back to the computer keyboard rhythmically tapping out a new configuration of keys. The red iridescence once again shivered. This time no hologram appeared. Instead, around the man and the woman each appeared a green aura from head to toe, glowing brightly. The technician then requested that the man and woman each review the kind of pleasant memories they had hoped would have permeated their entire relationship.

Each one separately began to review bits and pieces of memories from the time when they were first falling in love, and were first married. Pleasant memories and feelings filled their thoughts and bodies. The technician then instructed the man and the woman to interact in any way.

They turned to each other and they began to speak. The strangest things began to happen. No matter what they said or did they only had feelings like the ones they had when they were in love. Both experimented. They tried being insulting and mean, the result was always the same pleasant responses.

Finally, the technician pressed the appropriate keys and the red iridescence returned at the expense of the diminishing green glow. The technician spoke, "This option offers a future of varied behavior with a limited range of feelings. The advantage is of course that this removes all the unpleasant low spots in a relationship. It is however at the expense of any new highs." The man and the woman once again looked at each other with interest.

At this point the technician rose from the chair and signaled the man and the woman to follow. Both stood and followed the technician out the door of the little room. Once again they passed down long corridors lined with rooms until the technician turned sharply into one of them. The walls were lined with tubes about two feet in diameter and eight feet high. These were stacked one on top of the other, one right next to the other. There must have been tens of thousands in the room. Each one appeared to be made of some kind of glass and was filled with a red iridescent glow.

The technician looked at the awed faces of the man and the woman and spoke once again without emotion, "What you see here is the last option we will offer to you." The technician went over to one of the tubes and waved a hand in front of it. "If one of you is placed inside this tube you may, after sufficient programming live the life you believed you would have on the day you married. We need only scan your expectations on that day, program a module for you and your life's dreams will come true. You will only experience this, it will not really happen, but you will not be able to tell the difference. You will spend the rest of your days in what resembles a coma, while internally you will experience a full life. We will monitor your life support, and draw off any excess energy you produce to pay your way." The technician waved a hand again and the tube opened still glowing red. "This one has been programmed for a short demonstration." The technician gestured to the man.

The man cautiously entered, and the door closed behind him. A strange feeling came over the man. His head became light. Suddenly he found himself in the technocrat supervisor's office holding the woman's hand and he heard himself say with conviction, feeling the belief, and the truth of his words. "We have decided we no not need your services. We are going to make our own pleasurable future." Leaving together he looked into the woman's eyes, and knew no matter what, they would find and keep the love they both had shared. Three days of continued joy rich with good times good loving and caring communication, were experienced by the man furthering his conviction. He had forgotten he was in the tube when suddenly the environment around him dissolved and he was standing in a tube staring at the technician.

He stepped out and the woman was just stepping out of the tube next to his. They looked at each other. No words were spoken. Time resumed. The technician led them back to the technocrat supervisor's office and told them that they must now decide their fate. The technician left them alone.

In an hour the technocrat supervisor came into the office and asked, "What is your decision?"

The man and the woman looked at each other and finally the man said "We have decided not to use your services, however tempting they may be. We are going to try to build our own future out of the joys of our past and do a better job this time. If we fail we will return but do not expect us. We know now it will not be as easy as you can make it but we hope it will be better, than, you can make it." With that they turned and left.

The technocrat supervisor raised an eyebrow and turned to the wall behind him. A wave of his hand and the wall disappeared leaving technician 4 standing there. The technocrat supervisor walked up to the technician, and said, "Once again you succeeded. You are to be commended on this effort. Return now to your duties." The technician smiled, the technocrat supervisor smiled and the man and the woman lived happily ever after.

Introduction

And they lived happily ever after. Is this just a therapist's fairy-
tale? Certainly it does prescribe a most desirable solution. Rather
than deciding who is right or wrong or receding into the past or
living in an illusory future, these two people came to the best of
all solutions. One of generative experience where each of them
could generate behaviors towards one another that would elicit
their most desirable responses as well as respond to difficulties
such that they could become opportunities for enrichment. What's
more, they would do this independently with no need for a therapist's apron strings to hang on to. Of course this is only fiction, just
a story. Besides, just how specifically did these two people come
to this happy ending? Was it chance? Or the technician's trickery?
Or was there a deliberate plan? If there was, can you find it?

Now the technician had some very elaborate tools which produced some very elaborate affects. But could each of us produce
the same affects as well as the happy ending without such mechani-
cal wonders? I can. To do so you would need the Meta Techniques
of Change developed by my colleagues and me and the skills to use
them effectively. I know this to be true. I have used them to produce and sustain living happily ever after myself and to accomplish
such happy endings for those persons who have come to me seeking change. I'm very good at producing happily ever afters person-
ally and professionally because of my adept and creative use of the
Meta Techniques of Change. Those happy endings are available
to anyone who becomes skillfull in the use and application of these
techniques.

Although they have been taught internationally to professionals
in the field of psychology, this book is the first published description of many of those highly valued and sought after Techniques.
These methods of therapeutic intervention were developed over
a number of years through such endeavors as studying therapeutic
wizards like Fritz Perls, Virginia Satir, and Milton Erickson, M.D.,
doing therapy with individuals, couples and families and leading
training seminars for all manner of professional communicators.
Truly wizards themselves, Richard Bandler and John Grinder may
have through their books and personal contact, turned much of the
field of clinical psychology around to a different, more productive
direction. This different direction gives whole new perspectives on

old understandings and, most important, provides the actuality of achieving chosen desired results through therapeutic intervention. Each Meta Technique of Change provides a behavioral outcome that is easily verifiable in experience thus leaving no doubt about its validity. These techniques represent a tremendous advance in therapeutic technology.

In the beginning Richard Bandler and John Grinder combined their remarkable skills of detecting and utilizing patterns of human behavior to produce change and applied those skills to constructing a useful therapeutic model of the English language. They succeeded in creating the Meta-Model. (*The Structure Of Magic I,* Richard Bandler/John Grinder 1975)[1]. The Meta-Model is a specific set of linguistic strategies for responding in a useful and productive manner to the form of the verbalizations presented by people. It is also the foundation upon which the material in this book was built. (I have presented a distillation of the Meta-Model in appendix I for this reason and encourage you to use it.)

My own association with Richard Bandler and John Grinder goes back to pre Meta-Model days. That association began with extensive training experiences and expanded to complete professional collaboration. (The ultimate personal expression of these productive and satisfying years is my marriage to Richard.) Though I have acquired formal modeling skills through my years of doing research, seeing clients and conducting training seminars with Richard and John, my favorite activities remain to be the direct application of our methods in producing desired change and in teaching them to others. It is in these areas that my own creativity and personal style shine. As I teach this material in seminars I find it easy and pleasant to make the seemingly complicated techniques and patterns of human behavior understandable and learnable to even the layperson. Certainly this presentation will be a test of those teaching abilities. I mean to make the relevant patterns of human behavior and Meta Techniques of Change comprehensible and rich with experience by providing detailed descriptions and meaningful clinical examples. Each technique is presented in a step by step manner and some of them are suitable for self help.

My success in teaching you will be determined by your ability to take the material presented in this book and use it in your professional and personal lives. This will mean that I have assisted you in constructing the bridge between the form and the content of human behavior so necessary to effective therapeutic intervention in particular and effective communication in general.

The patterns of human behavior and the Meta Techniques of Change to be presented here are fascinating in and of themselves. However, the motivation to write this book comes instead from the many happy endings to seemingly impossible problems that are accomplished by their use. My personal bias about what constitutes a happy ending motivates me to present the application of this material to the context of sex therapy. (There is always some good loving in my happy endings.) This personal bias as well as my professional experience has led me to believe that persons functioning anywhere in the spectrum of the therapeutic professions have need of skills in dealing with the area of sexual expression.

For instance, a colleague and participant in many training sessions reported to me a case of a woman who came for treatment of torkillas, a condition involving the turning of the head into a fixed and rigid position, the person having almost no neck mobility. While treating this psychosomatic symptom, the therapist learned that its origin was an incident of forced fellatio at age eight. The turning away of the head had become the manifestation of the client's unconscious desire to avoid another such experience. Learning about the origin of this symptom was important to the treatment of her torkillas, but that traumatic episode also accounted for the client's present state of severe sexual dysfunction. So, although it was not her initial reason for coming to therapy, treating the present sexual dysfuntion was intrinsic to treating the symptomatic manifestation of torkillas. Thus, this case exemplifies the need for tools to do sex therapy that can also be integrated into an ongoing general treatment program.

As I travel widely conducting training seminars dealing with communication and change, I have come into contact with many persons practicing sex therapy. Some are highly regarded for their professional skills and do indeed help their clients to achieve richer sexual experiences. Yet, not infrequently, even these persons have approached me in a secretive manner to ask confidentially for help. In one case, a woman sex therapist could not achieve orgasm without the use of a vibrator. Another couldn't achieve orgasm during intercourse. A man who is a coordinator and teacher of courses in sexual functioning for both a medical school and a family therapy training center sought consultation because of periods of impotency. What does it mean when a significant number of those doing sex therapy and sex education themselves suffer from a sexual dysfunction?

Partially, this can be accounted for by the fact that human sexual behavior is often still treated as though it lies outside the spectrum of all other human behavior. Whether ignored or fully concentrated upon, it is a gross distortion to view sexuality apart from the totality of the human system.

The Structure of Experience

Understanding that human sexual behavior is but an aspect of a functioning system, involves more than merely appreciating the importance of a systemic approach to sex therapy. Human experience is generated as an interaction between what the external world provides for our senses to take in, and what our minds produce in the way of internally-generated imagery, internal dialogue, smells and feelings. Because the Meta Techniques of Change provide an understanding of this interaction, and for the use of skills appropriate to this interaction, I could, and did, assist the aforementioned persons in achieving the changes they desired in their sexual functioning.

We think in pictures, sounds, feelings, and words. When these internally-generated processes are not aligned with the sensory experience available to us from the world, a certain incongruity arises. This incongruity can be useful in some contexts. For example, we can daydream through long, boring meetings or place our consciousness on a pleasant memory or fantasy while enduring a visit to the dentist. These internal processes allow us to plan, remember the past, project into the future, but they can also limit our ability to achieve desired experiences.

I'm sure you are all familiar with those persons who stop themselves from doing anything new because they think "they will look silly". Specifically, they picture themselves doing the new behavior badly and feel embarrassed as though the picture had actually occurred. They then inhibit their behavior rather than risk experiencing the projected possible embarrassment.

Another example of internal processes distracting and limiting the actualization of desired experience is one most therapists are

familiar with; namely, the experience of having their work super-
vised at various levels of training. Often under such circumstances
the therapist under supervision is so distracted by internal projec-
tions of how the supervisor might be responding to his behavior
that the quality of his work diminishes radically.

In the context of sexual experiences, regardless of the quality of
foreplay and sexual expression, if either person is carrying on an
internal dialogue about tomorrow's shopping list or reciting multi-
plication tables, the intensity of the experience will be considerably
diminished. Similarly if while making love you were to picture
some conflicting scene (say, an argument with your mother) or
hear internal voices that distracted you from the ongoing experience (your mother's voice saying, "Now, nice girls don't do such
things," or your own voice saying, "I wonder if he/she is getting
tired.") or if you were to remember inappropriate feelings from
some past unrelated experience like taking an exam or driving
through traffic, the totality of the experience would be lost. In such
instances your experience would become an incongruent mixture
of the present lovemaking and other pictures, sounds, words, or
feelings not related to the present experience. Even when these
internally-generated processes are congruent with the ongoing
sexual experience they can still detract from the intensity of it.
Such as: if while making love you pictured each area of the body
touched by your right hand it is quite possible you would be more
aware of the images than of the feelings. Or if you constructed an
image of how you and your partner appeared to an unseen spectator from across the room you may lose all conscious awareness of
the body sensations caused from direct stimuli. To quote Bill Masters from *Pleasure Bond:*

> "There probably isn't anyone who, while having intercourse,
> doesn't become a spectator for a time. On occasion we watch
> what we ourselves may be doing or what our partner is doing.
> It's perfectly natural consciously to observe the procedure; in
> fact, it's quite stimulating to do this now and then. What is
> important is the degree to which we assume this spectator's role.
> In some cases, being the spectator on occasion may reflect a
> detachment from any emotional involvement. This, too, is na-
> ture and no cause for concern. But it does cut down on the input
> of the stimulus. For instance, if you are the spectator during

sexual activity, some degree of your wife's pleasure and excitement doesn't really get through to you, which means you lose
that stimulation. And to a degree your own pleasure is dulled
because you're not lost in the experience you're observing. I am
not saying that you experience no pleasure at all. I'm just saying
that some of it is blocked. A level of perception is blocked."[2]

These internal processes can also be utilized to enhance our
sexual experiences at times. Again, Bill Masters writes in *Pleasure
Bond;*

"All of us use fantasy to a greater or less degree. It is a form
of self-stimulation. It helps us move from where we are to where
we want to be, when the occasion warrants. In that sense it is a
bridge and can be very useful."[3]

Perhaps Bill Master's analogy of a bridge is especially appropriate here. In cases of sexual dysfunction internally generated experience often lies on one side of a wide and deep chasm while
external sensory experience lies on the other. If internal experience can be directed to produce desirable fantasies which are
somehow congruent with the ongoing external sensory experience
the chasm can be bridged and the two sides can come into alignment.

The Meta Techniques of Change presented here offer infinite
possibilities for constructing these bridges both *between* individuals
and *within* an individual. While building such bridges it is important to remember that our consciousness is a limited phenomenon.
As such our subjective experience is largely dependent upon just
what that consciousness is focused on. We are either conscious of
internal experience, external experience or a diluted mixture of
the two. While there are times when each of these is preferable the
diluted mixture of internal fantasy and external sex is a move
towards focusing full consciousness upon the intense externally
generated experiences the sexual encounter provides. This book
offers methods of building such bridges and ways to help others
and yourself across them.

The Needs to be fulfilled

Surely, it is impossible to overemphasize the contribution that satisfying sexual contact makes to the success of a relationship. Moments of shared physical intimacy in which two persons pleasure one another to fulfillment can provide a foundation for a relationship that external pressures and harassments find difficult to destroy. With pleasure inherent, naturally occurring sexual behavior serves to express passion, intimacy, love, tenderness and much more through direct experience. Though words may enhance, the vitality of the experience is carried by direct sensuous communication. The touches, smells, sounds and sights of lovemaking are profound means of communication from one person to another. How terrible it is that such natural and poignant human experiences are needlessly denied to any person.

There is a tremendous need for effectual methods in dealing with sexual dysfunction. Often people don't know whether they are functioning "normally" or not. "A conservative estimate," according to Masters and Johnson in *Human Sexual Inadequacy* "would indicate half the marriages are either presently sexually dysfunctional or imminently so in the future."[4] Sexual functioning is a unique area within the realm of psychotherapy. Whereas in most interactions with people the therapist has the freedom to interpret behavior as progress or relapse in relationship to psychological and interrelationship problems, sexual functioning has a quality whereby success or failure is directly demonstrable in sensory experience. Here the client's sensory experience is a definite demonstration of whether or not desired changes are taking place. Rather than this being the impetus for shying away, the therapist can look forward to the satisfaction of success such definitive feedback can bring.

In proceeding to present to you these patterns and techniques for accomplishing success (personal and professional happy endings) no lengthy definition of what clinically constitutes sexual dysfunction need be given. Masters and Johnson have already done that so splendidly in their books, that to do so here would only be redundant. Also there is such a proliferation of material offering explicit sex techniques, that attempting to offer anything new in that area, would most assuredly tax my creativity.

The material presented here will provide both a theoretical

frame work as well as specific therapeutic techniques for the purpose of enhancing the client's sexual experience. Universal in their application to human behavior, let it be emphasized that these techniques are only implicitly sexual because of the context in which they are presented here. Although presented for use within the context of sexual dysfunction, these patterns and the specific techniques associated with them are useful with any problem content. I sincerely urge you to generalize their use to other contexts. If you do, they can provide concepts of organization and methods of intervention that can be used by any person regardless of previous training.

To summarize then—while others have distilled patterns of human sexual behavior previously unknown, and developed effective treatment procedures for dealing with sexual dysfunction, there is still much room for improvement. The existing procedures are less effective with phobic responses that are the consequences of earlier traumas or severe conditioning. Most existing procedures can hardly be used with the severely disturbed individual or one not involved in a couple relationship. They are especially inadequate when internally generated experience interferes with the natural sequence of physiological responses that occur in a successful sexual experience. This is by no means a criticism of existing treatment procedures. Quite to the contrary, the fact is that the existing body of knowledge developed by Masters and Johnson and others has diminished the need to further develop skills in this area, but it has not abolished it. There is no point in rejecting what others have done however there is a point in adding to it. I doubt strongly that they would want anyone to stop where they have paused, but instead would be eager to add new choices to their own procedures. Two ways of accomplishing this are: (1) utilizing the patterns of human behavior and the Meta Techniques of Change, proved so very effective in changing the human experience in general, in the field of sex therapy, and (2) integrating sex therapy as a field into the treatment of the person as a whole rather than separating it from the rest of human experience. Likewise during your own process of evolving and integrating the new choices offered in this book, I respectfully ask you to keep all the useful choices that are already in your behavior and merely add to them. Do keep in mind that yesterday's science fiction is today's science and that not all technology is built of machines. You can open the doorway to becoming an experience technician with the pages that follow.

Strategic Overview

You can use the following material to guide your behavior while assiting people in developing strategies, at the unconscious level that will help them to generate sexual experiences more satisfying and enriching than before. The sequence of the material provides a structure that can be used to explicitly organize behavior in a way that allows therapists to act effectively in dealing with human sexual dysfunction.

For this presentation to be useful it must reduce the complexity of successful therapeutic intervention to a degree that we are able to handle. I have worked diligently to keep that requirement in mind throughout this presentation. While offering numerous techniques for successful therapeutic intervention, the patterns are presented in simple, easy-to-follow steps with several examples to further elucidate these procedures. These patterns of communication and change have been used by my colleagues and me, as well as taught to psychotherapists in training workshops all over the country, always with great success. It is my experience that when therapists are careful to make the necessary distinctions, and to organize their experience as to sequence and category as prescribed here, then they are consistently effective in assisting their clients in reaching desired goals.

The form of this book is itself a strategy. This strategy, I have found, is a useful way to organize my behavior in accomplishing any desired goals. It has three basic steps which are:

I. Gathering information concerning the client's present state and desired state and establishing rapport with client/s.
II. Evolving the client/s from their present state to their desired state.
III. Futurepacing—integrating the desired state experience into their ongoing behavior.[5]

These three steps construct effective therapeutic change, when two vital ingredients are added: sensory experience and flexibility of behavior. The external sensory experience to detect what observable behaviors constitute the present or problem state and what observable behaviors would constitute the desired or cured state for any individual or couple. Once this is known it takes flexibility of behavior to move the client/s from where they are to where they want to be. If you are flexible in your behavior you can shift from one method of intervention to another until one achieves the desired results. Again in other words the steps are:

I. Find out *gracefully* where clients want to go and where they are now.
II. Pick a method of getting to that desired state and use it.
III. Notice whether the desired destination has indeed been reached. If yes, then take measures to insure that it can be reached in the future without you. If the desired destination has not been reached then go back to step II and pick another method and use it—continuing to use different methods until success is achieved.

This may sound like an incredible oversimplification of the very complex activity of doing therapy, yet it is for me the most elegant possible organization of behavior while doing therapy. Again this strategy constitutes the *form* of this book. The content of this book concerns itself with:

A. What information concerning the client's present state and desired state is vital to gather with your senses.
B. How to gather it.
C. Methods of establishing rapport consistently and meaningfully with any and all clients.
D. Techniques of evolving the client from present state to desired state.
E. Methods of how to effectively *futurepace* the learnings and experiences accomplished within the therapy session into the client's ongoing behavior.

As with any book the form and content of this text is a representation of the author. This is how I have come to be organized. It is with this strategy and these methods of intervention that I change myself and those who come to me seeking change.

It can be likened to building someone a new house. I learn about the existing structure and what is desired in the new one. Do they want doors with locks or open arches for coming and going? Large

open communal spaces or cozy cubby holes for privacy? What do
they want to see, hear, and feel in their new dwelling that is not
available to them now? And what aspects of their present home
would they like to keep intact and integrate into the new one?

Once I know all of this I can choose the materials and tools
suitable for constructing that new house. And I have enough of a
variety of materials and tools that I can adjust from what doesn't
work to what does. While construction is under way I'm careful to
build in endurance to insure the lasting quality of their new home.
All the while I take care to install possibilities for future expansion
should such a need or desire arise.

Each of these "Dwellings" is built upon the foundation of my
own personal philosophies. Included in those is the belief that
each human being has somewhere within him all the resources that
are needed to accomplish any change. My primary function is to
access and organize those resources in such a way as to produce
lasting and desired change. I'm a believer in the possibilities of
human experience rather than in the limitations.

The information and techniques of intervention presented in
this book have made it possible for me to actualize my good intentions and personal philosophies. It is towards the actualizations of
your own good intentions I would now like to move you.

Notes

1. Bandler and Grinder *The Structure of Magic* Vol. I, (Palo Alto, Calif: Science and Behavior Books., 1975)
2. W. H. Masters and V. E. Johnson, *The Pleasure Bond* (New York: Bantam Books, 1975) p. 33
3. Ibid p. 76
4. W.H. Masters and V.E. Johnson, *Human Sexual Inadequacy* (Boston: Little, Brown and Co., 1970), p. 27
5. Futurepacing—Since building in endurance must often be done throughout the therapy process, it is usually integrated into the specific therapeutic intervention rather than being a seperate intervention. I will however devote a section to the concept of futurepacing to emphasize its importance in producing lasting change.

Part II

Gathering Information
and
Establishing Rapport

This section begins the presentation of what information is important to gather to understand the client's present and desired states.

Representational Systems

There are those clinicians who say sexual dysfunction is not the problem and instead treat the relationship as the problem. But what does it mean for a relationship to have problems? The word "relationship" is itself a distortion of the process word "relate". That is, there is no tangible object called a relationship instead it is a process made up of animate beings relating to each other. Now clinicians might suggest that caring and trust make a relationship work. But, really, what is "caring" and what specifically is "trust"? As such, they are merely words implying events that have not been defined as to how they occur in a particular person's experience. If we denominalize "the relationship" it becomes the verb "relate" and we can ask the questions "who is relating to whom and how are they relating to each other that brings about unhappiness and dissatisfaction? How can they relate to one another in ways that generate more desirable experiences. The answers to these questions give useful information as to just what the client's present and desired states are.

Most often it is easy to detect when people are not relating well to each other. They tell you and they tell you verbally as well as nonverbally. Their verbalizations are representations of their experiences, just as maps are representations of territories. People use words to talk about what they "believe" happened. They can never tell you what actually happened, just as a map can never be

33

a complete representation of the territory of which it is a model. Thus a most important thing for those of us in the business of communication to understand is, that what people tell us is *not* what actually happened, but instead, what they consciously experienced as happening. There is a tremendous difference between the two. So, if two individuals come in telling two different stories about the same phenomenon, I know they are both right. Typically it is not that one is telling the truth and the other is lying. They are each telling about what they are conscious of in respect to what they experienced.

The content of people's verbalizations tell you what they believe. The process of people's verbalizations tell you how they created those beliefs. Almost every couple coming in for therapy disagree about what takes place between them. . . . he says "f" and "h" happened and she says it is more like "m" and "n". Noticing how their descriptions differ is important to understanding how they miscommunicate. It is here at the process level of their communications that we begin to find the answers to questions of how best to direct the process of change. The words each of us use to express ourselves are indicators of the elements of our conscious experience and thus can begin to point the way out of dissatisfaction and towards fulfillment.

Suppose your client comes in and says,

"Well, the way things look to me is that . . ., I really can't see any future in our marriage. I am willing to try because the way I see myself is as a person who is very concerned, but I really can't imagine that things will get better. It is just too dark and gloomy."

And his wife says,

"Well, I really feel that things can be better. We have a lot to build upon and if we work on our relationship and try very hard we can smooth out our difficulties."

While listening to this communication, if we pay attention to *what* they say and take the *content* as being important—that he doesn't believe it will work out and she does—then we have to start guessing that one of them is right and the other wrong. If you deal with the content, you don't find out anything about the *process* by which they disagree. You don't learn how they came to represent the experience of their marriage as, on one hand, being hopeless and on the other promising. Instead you are limited to responding only to their verbalizations by forming judgments, opinions and interpretations of them as if their descriptions were real world experiences. If you *believe* either her or him, you are responding to the content of what they are talking about and this puts you in the same mess they are in with each other. This happens because the degree to which you can "really understand" is the degree to which you can respond to the *form* of their verbalizations. They can't understand each other; they disagree about what reality is. Your job as a professional communicator is not to concern yourself with "reality"; your job is to concern yourself with process.

How is it, then, that two people who live together disagree so much? By observing closely the process that's involved in just their sentences, the first thing you will notice is that they are talking about different portions of the same experience of the world. He's talking purely in pictures, about images he sees or doesn't see internally. That is, not just things he sees or doesn't see in the outside world of sensory experience, but internally-generated images. She, on the other hand, is talking about feelings. The way you can identify this is by noting the process words in the sentence. If you attend to the nouns in the sentence you get caught in content. If you attend to the process words—the adjectives, verbs and adverbs—you identify something about the process. All the process words in his sentences have to do with making pictures—"look," "see," "imagine,"—all words presupposing seeing. And, all her words have to do with making feelings internally—"feel," "hard," "smooth" all words presupposing feelings. This immediately tells you that they are both describing internally generated experiences about the condition of their marriage. It also tells you that they are each aware of, and talking about different portions of their experience: he, the visual portion; and she, the kinesthetic (or feeling dimension). This indicates that there is an important difference in how these people organize and express their perceptions. This difference in the organization and expression of their perceptions is *how* they don't get along. This is in fact the process by which most miscommunication takes place. It is as though two different languages were being spoken but nobody noticed.

So, what does it mean to relate to a person in a "successful" way? Partly, it means talking about the same portions of experiences at the same moment in time. To illustrate this, here is an example taken directly from a therapy transcript:

Shirley: I just really don't like how he is always pawing me in public. He makes a scene and doesn't even see how everyone looks at us. It just attracts a lot of attention and I want him to show me more respect in front of other people.

Bob: But I like to be close to her. I want to make contact with her when I'm feeling affectionate and sometimes I feel affectionate outside of closed doors. She pushes me away and I think that's really cold to do to someone you're supposed to love. She used to like my reaching for her. Now, I don't feel appreciated by her at all.

Again, the words used by Bob and Shirley indicate that they are aware of two very different experiences concerning his touching her in public. It's not that one is "right" and the other "wrong." Looking at the process words allows us to make useful distinctions about what portion of experience they are each conscious of. Her words—"scene," "see," "show," "looks" all presuppose a *visual* representational system.[5] His words—"contact," "feel," "pushes," "cold," "reaching"—all presuppose a *kinesthetic* representation. Their words indicate that they are each attending to a different portion of experience: she, the visual portion; he, the kinesthetic portion. Until these people speak a similar language, they can't hope to communicate with each other successfully.

You see we can only be conscious of a small portion of our ongoing experience. Even now as you read this sentence you could be aware of the sounds around you, the quality of the air you are breathing, the type of print you are reading, the color of the margins or the weight and position of your left hand. As you read each of these possibilities it is likely you shifted your conscious awareness to what was being suggested. It is very unlikely that you would have been consciously aware of all or even any of the parameters of experience I directed you to. It has been postulated that human consciousness can handle seven plus or minus two chunks of information at a time. This means that we direct our conscious awareness to certain portions of our ongoing experience. What portions of experience you bring into consciousness is determined by an interaction of your present motivations and childhood learnings.

If you attend a lecture given by an erudite and fascinating

speaker it is unlikely that you will be conscious of the color of shoes and dress of the stranger sitting two seats away. Your attention will be on the speaker. If, however, the speaker is a bore, you may become aware of feelings of loneliness which motivate you to look about for possible persons to make a personal connection with. In which case you may become very aware of the color of shoes and dress worn by that stranger. Thus your present motivation would determine what aspects of your experience you brought into conscious awareness.

As a child you learned to value some aspects of the communications your family presented you with over others. If your mother told you "Everything is ok" but had clenched teeth and fists as well as tears in her eyes, which message did you trust? The one you heard or the one you saw? If your father scolded you verbally about some behavioral misdemeanor but smiled jovially and slapped you on the back as he did so, which message did you believe? A child from a family such as this would predictably come to value and thus attend to the visual portions of experience over others. He or she would be aware of what they see more than what the words told them. If told "I love you" they might reply "But you don't *look* like you love me. How can I believe you?"

As a listener, you can discern what portion of experience a person is representing consciously by attending to the process words used. Such words usually specify a process of seeing, hearing, feeling, and smelling or tasting. The following are some examples of such process words:

Visual	*Auditory*	*Kinesthetic*	*Smells, Tastes*
picture	scream	feel	bitter
vague	hear	warm	salty
bright	screech	touch	fragrant
flash	shout	handle	pungent
blue	loud	grasp	smells
see	amplify	soft	stale
focus	tune	tight	fresh
perspective	tone	smooth	taste
clear	harmonize	rough	sweet
			sour

Listening to any verbalization as well as reading transcripts of couple counseling, sex counseling, etc., can provide you with a wealth of pertinent examples of these representational systems. While researching transcripts, I became aware of an interesting phenomenon; namely, that married persons who participated in extramarital affairs typically referred to their marital relationship in kinesthetic predicates—solid, stuck, cemented, etc.—and to their extramarital affairs with visual predicates—how they were attracted by what they saw, that these relationships were more colorful, etc. Also, in reading transcripts of persons who considered themselves as swingers and who participated in group sex, I found a proliferation of gustatory predicates. They likened sexual intercourse with going out to dinner; stated that, like gourmets, they sought varieties in cuisine and found the thought of monogamy bland and tasteless.

Process words that do not indicate any of these four parameters of experience are *unspecified*. That is, they are unspecified as to just how the process is being represented or executed—whether in pictures, smells, feelings or sounds. Some examples of unspecified predicates are:

think	learn	change	consider
know	nice	respectful	remember
understand	intuit	trusting	believe

When presented with such words, the listener therapist has several options for discerning how, specifically, the process is being represented. You can ask, "How, *specifically*, do you think (know) (understand) (learn)?" This will elicit either a verbal response richer in process details or it will elicit nonverbal behavior (eye scanning patterns) which will specify internal process. Of course, people do not consciously sort through and choose the words or syntax that they use to describe their experience. However, their words are a representation of what, out of all the experience available to them, they are conscious of.

Accessing Cues

So while a person's language gives us information concerning the speaker's conscious experience we must look elsewhere for information concerning *how* the specific experience came into their consciousness. Most often in the therapeutic context people are speaking of their past or their internal experience. The client seldom speaks about his current experience: the color of the therapist's chair, the weight of his own arm resting on his thigh, the sounds of the ventilation equipment or any sensory experiences which are occurring as he is sitting there in your office. Rather the client speaks of internal responses to the present therapeutic activities or internal representations of past or projected future events.

In order to speak of such internally generated experiences each of us must in some way, gain access to those internal experiences. To further illustrate this point I would like you to do the following:

1. Think of a pleasant childhood experience you shared with a friend.
2. Remember what clothes you wore as you graduated from highschool.
3. Remember your first french kiss.
4. Remember a time when your curiosity overcame your fears.

In order to accomplish any of these tasks it was necessary for you to make accessible certain distinct classes of past experiences. How you obtained the information is referred to by my colleagues and me as accessing. (The process of going and getting information internally i.e., pictures, sounds, words, feelings which make up memories, fantasies, etc.). Those specific nonverbal behaviors which give information about how you make such experiential information available to your conscious mind are called *accessing cues*.

You see, besides words and syntax, people offer to the careful observer-listener a plethora of meaningful nonverbal behavior that is also generated unconsciously. There has been much speculation and interpretation concerning human nonverbal behavior or "body language" (witness the many irresponsible interpretations of what it means if a woman's legs are crossed or not, etc.). I believe that some of the most relevant information concerning nonverbal behavior is provided by the concept of *assessing cues*. My colleagues, John Grinder, Richard Bandler, Judith DeLozier and I found in the course of our studies of human behavior that eye scanning patterns were definitely related to the internal processing necessary to bring into consciousness information regarding internal, past, or future experiences.

As stated in Patterns II: . . . each of us has developed particular body movements which indicate to the astute observer which representational system we are using. Especially rich in significance are the eye scanning patterns which we have developed. Thus, for the student of hypnosis, predicates in the verbal system and eye scanning patterns in the nonverbal system offer quick and powerful ways of determining which of the potential meaning making resources—the representational systems—the client is using at a moment in time, and therefore how to respond creatively to the client. Consider, for example, how many times you have asked someone a question and they have paused, said: "Hmmmmm, let's see" and accompanying this verbalization, they move their eyes up and to the left. Movement of the eyes up and to the left stimulates (in right handed people) eidetic images located in the non dominant hemisphere. The neurological pathways that come from the left side of both eyes (left visual fields) are represented in the right cerebral hemisphere (non dominant). The eye scanning movement up and to the left is a common way people use to stimulate that hemisphere as a method for accessing visual memory. Eye movements up and to the right conversely stimulate the left cerebral hemisphere and constructed images—that is, visual representations of things that the person has never seen before (see *Patterns*, volume II, page 182).

. . . accessing cues which may be detected visually. Specifically (for the right handed person):

accessing cue	*representational system indicated*		
eyes up and to the left	eidetic imagery	(V)	(visual)
eyes up and to the right	constructed imagery	(V)	(visual)
eyes defocused in position	imagery	(V)	(visual)
eyes down and to the left	auditory internal	(A)	(auditory)

telephone postures	auditory internal	(A) (auditory)
eyes left or right, same		
level of gaze	auditory internal	(A) (auditory)
eyes down and to the		
right	kinesthetics	(K) (kinesthetic)

To further illustrate: As you face the person you are communicating with and their eyes move in the direction shown in these "happy face" drawings the internal process designated is being accessed.

Specifically (for the right handed person)

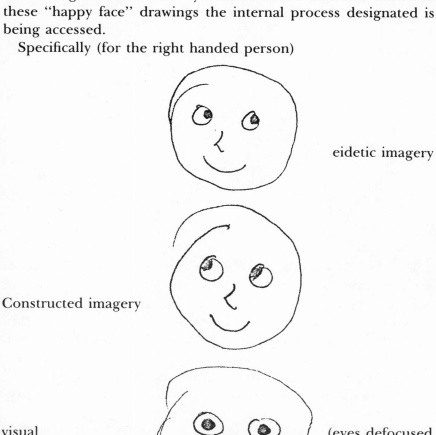

eidetic imagery

Constructed imagery

visual
imagery
could be eidetic
or constructed)

(eyes defocused
fixed position
usually some
pupil dilation)

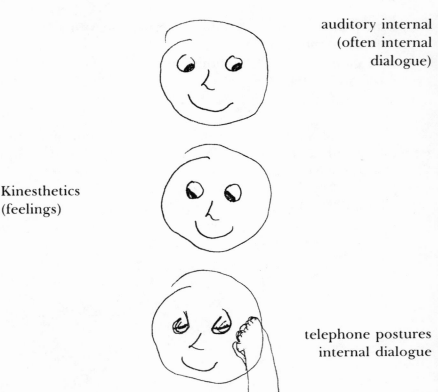

auditory internal
(often internal
dialogue)

Kinesthetics
(feelings)

telephone postures
internal dialogue

You probably have had the experience of asking a question of someone who then broke eye contact, shifted their eyes up and left, and said, "Hmmm, let's *see*" and they did. At other times, though, their eyes possibly went up and right or defocused while they stared straight ahead, or shifted down and left or down and right, or perhaps some sequence of these eye scanning movements occurred. You may not have known it, but that person was indicating to you *how* they were accessing the needed information to answer your question.

Miscommunication generated from a lack of understanding about accessing cues is rampant. When accessing, people are not "in" sensory experience and, therefore, they miss sensory input. Thus, the therapist or people helper hears the frequent complaints:

"He just doesn't listen to me. He's right there in the room and I tell him something and then he pretends he never heard me." (This woman failed to notice when her husband was actually available to *consciously* receive information. Though he was in the room with her and even maintaining eye contact, his pupils were dilated indicating visualization.)

"You did not tell me that. I never heard you say any such thing." (And he's right. He didn't hear her say any such thing.)

"Didn't you see where I put it? You were right there." "No, I wasn't. You did not put it down while I was there." (And they are both right, because his conscious mind was attending to his internal images rather than to what was going on in his external experience.)

When a human being's consciousness is attending to internal processes, visual, auditory and even kinesthetic, *input* often goes unnoticed. If it is above a certain threshold, it will bring the person back out to sensory experience; otherwise, the sensory input will go in but may not be available to that person consciously. Thus, I teach people in couples, families, groups, even business organizations, how to tell—by watching—whether a person is consciously listening, seeing, etc.

There is a certain handicap involved in writing about nonverbal communication in that it is more easily demonstrated visually. This being so, you will be "limited" to verifying some of the material presented here by having to find it in your own experience of relating to others and, the sooner, the better.

The following are examples of accessing cues, including the relevant eye-scanning patterns:

Sue: "I just can't see it (eyes up, left). John has never been able to do it before, why should he start now?"

John: "Did you hear that (eyes down, left)? I ask myself, 'Why bother even trying?' It seems like (eyes down, right) there's just no pleasing her."

(In this example, Sue is making eidetic images. Naturally, she can't see what hasn't occurred in the past. It would be important to help her build a constructed image of John doing what he hasn't yet done in order for her to feel hopeful about the future possibilities.)

Or,

Will: "Do you see how she's dressed? I remember (eyes up, left) how she used to look. If she loved me, she wouldn't let herself go to pot like that. I see myself (eyes up, right) as an attractive man, and it's embarrassing (eyes up, right). Of course, I wouldn't say this in front of her."

(Will compares a past image of his wife with her present appearance, then constructs images of how he sees himself and how others see them. Throughout, he is comparing what he sees in sensory experience with his internal images, and the sensory experience comes in a poor second.

Or, from a women's rap group:

Sal: (Eyes up, left) "He's too fast. I put on a negligee and light a candle, turn back the sheets, get all ready and he doesn't even notice (eyes up, left). He'd rather just grab for me in the night."
Stella: (Eyes down, right) "I wish Jim would just reach for me. I feel (down, right) so pressured all the time to perform and dress up and look just so (down, right). I get tired."
June: (Down, left) "That's not important. What's important is the (up, right) essence of how you approach each other. That you do it in love (up, right) as well as lust (down, right)."

(Sal is accessing past images and places an importance on visual aspects of the lovemaking experience. Stella expresses kinesthetic priorities which are congruent with her kinesthetic accessing cues. June's accessing cues indicate that she tells herself something internally, makes a constructed image concerning the "essence of how you approach each other," and then accesses kinesthetically in reference to the experience of lust.)

While using your ears to detect the words which indicate a person's representational system you can use your eyes to notice the client's accessing cues. Accessing cues are those eye movements that indicate *how* the client is thinking—in pictures, words, or feelings. These give us vital information concerning the internal behaviors of the client. Although we cannot know what the pictures or words or feelings are, we can tell what internal processes are being used to generate the person's overall experience.

Lead System

Just as people typically favor one representational system: as heard in the process words they most often use, so do people typically favor one internal process for accessing over others. The observant communicator can determine which internal process this is by noting which accessing cue is habitually used first. This favored internal process is referred to as the lead system.

In a recent workshop I brought two men up before the audience. Having discerned previously by their behavior that they processed information very differently from one another I used them to illustrate the concept of different lead systems. Asking the audience to watch them closely I instructed these men to merely think of the answers to the questions I was about to ask them. I then proceeded to ask a series of questions.

"What color are your mother's eyes?"
"How many doors in your house?"
"Which door slams the loudest?"
"Where is reverse in your car's gears?"
"How does it feel to be sunburned?"
"Can you hear your mother calling your name?"

One man looked first down and to his right in response to each question. The other looked first up and to his left in response to each question. The first searching kinesthetically for the answers while the other searched visually. They both found the answers to each question but they used different systems of accessing to do so. They used their own most typical lead system.

While some people's accessing cues would have varied with each question, these gentlemen's did not. That is why I chose them to illustrate lead system behavior. Rather than accessing visually for a question which asked for visual information—color—or auditorily for one that asked for sound—loudness, mother's voice —or kinesthetically for the feeling of being sunburned they each habitually accessed one internal process to answer each [of the questions.]

The following is their own descriptions of their internal experience in response to some of the questions.

Question I

Man I—I got the feeling of my mother then I saw her face and looked at her eyes.
Man II—I just saw her face and focused on her eyes.

Question II

Man I—I walked through my house starting at the front door and counted the doors on my fingers.

Man II—I saw pictures of the doors in my house like index cards and they just flipped in front of me and each card was numbered.

Question III

Man I—I felt myself slamming each one and listened
Man II—I saw each one slam and heard them.

Question VI

Man I—I just felt my skin turn hot and sensitive and it tightened.
Man II—I saw my face in a mirror and it was all red.

Their descriptions tell how they use one system to lead them to information contained in other modalities of experience. These two people would be apt to remember a shared experience differently by recalling and expressing it through differing sensory modalities. Their descriptions show how internally generated experience is influenced by what lead system is used.

In treating sexual dysfunction there is one lead system in particular to watch for. It is the constructed visual lead system and the accessing cue is up and right. Often, not always, but often the person who habitually accesses constructed images see themselves in their internal pictures. When asked to remember being kissed they see themselves being kissed rather than seeing the persons face approaching and feeling their lips making contact. An example of what such internal processing can mean in the sexual context is provided by Masters and Johnson.

"As sex play is introduced and mutual attempts made by marital partners to force an erective response, the impotent husband finds himself a spectator to his own sexual exchange. He mentally is observing his and his partner's response (or lack of it) to sexual stimulation. Will there be an erection? If and when the penis begins to engorge, how full will the erection become? When erection is obtained, how long will it last? The involuntary spectator in the room demands immediate answers for these questions from the anxious man in the bed, so intensely con-

cerned with his fears of sexual performance. Rather than allowing himself to relax, enjoy sexual stimulation, and permit his
natural sexual responsivity to create and maintain the erective
process, he as a spectator demands instant performance. In the
spectator role, a dysfunctional man completely negates any concept of natural sexual function. He cannot conceive of involuntary sexual responsivity sustaining an erection as a natural physiological process on the same natural plane as that of his
involuntary respiratory responsivity sustaining his breathing
mechanism.

Not only is there at least one spectator in the impotent male's
bedroom, frequently there are two. For the wife, who is physically attempting to provide her husband with an erection, simultaneously may be mentally occupying an equal position of watch-
fulness, critically observing the apprehensive male's level of
sexual responsivity. Is there to be an erection? If so, how full an
erection? Will it be usable? Will it be maintained? Is she stimulating her husband satisfactorily? If he obviously isn't responding, what could she be doing that is wrong? All these questions
arise when, in her spectator role, the wife quietly observes the
progress of the particular sexual episode in her marriage. Is it
any wonder that the wife of the impotent male usually is not fully
sexually responsive herself, even when the occasional sexual
opportunity presents? Even in the immediacy of sexual opportunity, she frequently is psychologically caught in the corner observing the physical proceedings rather than physiologically tied
to the bed totally involved with her own mating.

Neither partner realizes that the other is mentally standing in
an opposite corner, observing the marital bedding scene in a
spectator role. Both partners involuntarily distract themselves in
their spectator roles, essentially uninvolved in the experience in
which they are involved, to such an extent that there is no possibility for effective sexual stimuli to penetrate the impervious
layers of performance fear and involuntary voyeurism.[3]"

If you detect a person using a constructed image lead system
while asking them questions about past or anticipated future sexual experiences ask them directly if they see themselves in the
picture or do they see the experience as though they were inside

it (1st person). If they are seeing themselves you can use the process of overlaping representational systems to assist them in stepping into the picture and experiencing it more fully.

In the Therapy Context

To point up how useful it is to attend to representational systems and accessing cues, the following partial transcript is provided:

JoAnn is twenty-eight years old and has been referred by a former client who is her co-worker. She is an assistant fashion buyer for a small, but prestigious, women's clothing store. JoAnn is strikingly attractive—tall, slim, immaculately dressed and coifed: "picture perfect." (As the reader will note, sexual dysfunction was not the primary reason for the client entering therapy, but became important to the change process.)

Th: JoAnn, tell me, what is it that you hope to change for yourself?

C: (Eyes up, right) Well, I just see myself[1] being depressed too much of the time.

[1]accessing cue constructed image; visual predicate (see); internal response "depressed" (*)

Th: Depressed about what?

C: (Eyes up, left; left hand gestures)[2] Mostly my husband.

[2]edidetic visual accessing cue

Th: What do you see concerning your husband that you find depressing?

C: Well, (eyes up, left)[3] I don't know. He's not even around any more.

[3]eidetic visual accessing cue

Th: Oh. Does his being out of the picture depress you?

C: Yeah. (Eyes up and left).[4] Hmmm, it's just that he left me and I'm alone now.

[4]eidetic visual accessing cue

Th: That's how you see it, huh? He left you?

C: Oh, yeah. There's no two ways about it. *He* left me. I didn't want to split up.

Th: When did this happen?

C: (Eyes up, left)[5] Two years ago.

[5] eidetic visual accessing cue

Th: How would you like your experience to be?

C: (Eyes up, right; down, left)[6] I don't know. Not depressed.

[6] constructed image, then auditory accessing cue

Th: I'm wondering if you could tell me how you *want* your experience to be.

C: Well, (eyes up, left)[7], if I could just be happy again.

[7] visual eidetic image

Th: What do you see that could make you happy?

C: (Frowns) Hmmm (eyes up, left) If things were like they were.

Th: (Smiling) And just how were they then? (Leads her eyes back to up-left by shifting own eyes up-right.)

C: Oh, no. I don't want that (eyes up and left; eyes up, right). I'd be happy if I could see I was making progress.

Th: What would you need to see happening to know you were making progress?

C: Mostly relationship stuff (eyes up, left) . . . men.

Th: What men, specifically?

C: Any man (up left and up right).

Th: ANY MAN?

C: Well, no. But I don't have anyone really special.

Th: A woman as pretty as you are doesn't have men in her life?

C: There are men (up-left and down-right), but none special. Actually, I don't like men much (makes face).

Th: Oh, do you like women? (analogue gesture, eyebrows lift, etc., sexual connotation.)

As this transcript proceeds it becomes evident how knowledge of accessing cues and predicates allows the therapist to move with the client in useful and appropriate directions.

Along with utilizing predicates and accessing cues, the Meta-model is used throughout this transcript. For further discussion of the Meta-model, see appendix I.

C: No! God, no!

Th: Okay, okay. What do you mean you don't like men?

C: My husband used to accuse me of being lesbian.

Th: Oh, I'm sure you have ideas about what prompted such an accusation. I mean, your response was certainly adamant enough. But first I need to know what specifically would you need to see happening to know you are making progress.

C: I'd need to know I could make it work with a man (eyes up-right, frown).

Th: What does it mean to make it work?

C: That's not very clear to me.

Th: Well, use your imagination and paint a scene that would depict your making it work with a man.

C: (Eyes up, left; up, right; back left, than right, hold.)

Th: Can you imagine it?

C: Um Hmmm.

Th: (Reaching out, touching the client to reinforce the experience and *to associate* this particular touch with the experience.) Keep looking at that scene so it becomes clear to you just what you're setting your sights for.

C: It's kind of vague. I can't really see him clearly. Just me, but I know there's a man there. Mostly I know he loves me and he's pleased with me.

Th: Okay (removes hand). JoAnn, come back here. Hello. Now, what stops you from getting what's in that picture? You are certainly attractive enough to have men approach you. True?

C: Well, yes. But I can't keep them
      . . . I don't know. I'm just so depressed
      (eyes down, right).

You can see that attending to representational systems predicates and accessing cues helped to gather pertinent information as well as establish rapport with JoAnn.

As the session proceeded, JoAnn concluded that a central facet of her problem was her own sexual dysfunction. She went on to specify that most of all she wanted a successful relationship with a man and necessary to that success was having intimate sexual experiences that were pleasurable and satisfying which they had never been for her. While there was an abundance of opportunities for her to experience sexual encounters, she knew that some "things" had to change before utilizing them would do her any good. But at the time she did not know what "things" could or should be changed.

This demonstrates some of the content of JoAnn's problem. As well as obvious process information concerning JoAnn and her habitual use of a visual lead system and a visual representational system. Since, sexual functioning is primarily a kinesthetic experience, it was necessary to increase the flexibility of JoAnn's behavior to include, in consciousness, the kinesthetic parameters of internal and external experience in order for her to achieve the changes she wished.

Since consciousness is a limited phenomenon, if our consciousness is placed other than on the kinesthetic portion of experience during sexual activity, problems can often arise. Most highly visual people are flexible enough to switch to a kinesthetic representation during sexual encounters. If their most typical lead system is visual, they may be dependent upon sexually stimulating visual input to stimulate their responsivity, or perhaps they may utilize internally-generated visual images to accomplish the same thing. It is important to stress that "visuals" feel as much as anyone else, but they may not be conscious of those feelings unless they shift their attention to that aspect of experience. Where sex is concerned, most do.

In my experience, I have found that when a person habitually brings only one system into consciousness often all the "crap" is stored in another system. When that other system is kinesthetic and it is brought to consciousness there are only bad feelings; or, for the "kino," whose visual system is rarely if ever accessed there are only terrifying pictures. Thus, they unconsciously avoid bringing that system into consciousness as a way of protecting themselves. In such cases, a person's rigidity in using one system is the very best choice they presently have available to them.

Typical of this is a case of a young man I saw because of a decade-long history of migraine headaches. Like JoAnn, he accessed and represented visually despite the intrinsically kinesthetic nature of the questions asked. Except for the horrible headaches, he "drew a blank" where feelings were concerned. His entire head, neck and facial asymmetry were indicative of his habitual visual accessing (i.e., the right side of his face longer, left side shorter; left nostril shorter and higher; left side of mouth higher than the right; head forward and bent, chin up so that the back of his neck was constricted from habitually looking up; narrow chest and shoulders; breathing high in chest; eyebrows lifted, compressing his forehead; lines from squinting to focus internal pictures). Similar physical patterns could also be observed with JoAnn.

I literally moved his head and neck with my hands, and told him where to put his eyes in order to elicit a kinesthetic response. When asked, "What is there?," he replied, "Sadness," and the tears welled up in his eyes. Merely changing his head position caused the sadness to "disappear" (his words), but upon each readjustment to the kinesthetic accessing position, the sadness and tears returned. I employed the same technique with him as described in the next section with JoAnn, with equally effective therapeutic results. He had not been conscious of feelings unless they were overwhelmingly bad, as with the headaches. Once able to comfortably access kinesthetically, he could receive and respond to messages from his body about situations and activities that were headache-producing. Thus, he could intervene and generate responses to the stimuli that were much more beneficial than the headaches had been.

With JoAnn, throughout the first session she remained fixedly in a visual lead and representational system, alternating between eidetic (up and left) and constructed (up and right) images. This was so despite asking such questions as:

Th: And as you remember his words, how do you *feel?*

C: I just *see* myself as a failure.

Th: When do you *feel* really sexy?

C: I know I'm *sexy.* Lots of men want me. I just don't enjoy it.

Th: What do you remember most about sex with your husband?

C: The little sparkly things in the ceiling; I just waited for it to be over.

Th: What kind of sexual preferences do you have?

C: The lights out; it has to be dark.

When Lead and Representational Systems Differ

Another important distinction to be made is whether lead systems are inside or outside of the individual's conscious awareness. That is, whether a person can see his own internally-generated pictures, feel internally-generated feelings, hear internally-generated sounds or words. Often, with people who come into therapy, one system will lie outside of consciousness. This was the case in the "headache" example related above.

When the system outside of consciousness is the one that typically generates their experience, (is their lead system) it becomes impossible for the individual to have choices concerning what kinds of experiences are internally-generated. This occurs more often when there is a difference between lead system and representational system than when they are the same.

As you listen to people's predicates and watch their accessing cues you will notice that sometimes they do not match. That is, they access visually and talk about their feelings or access kinesthetically and tell you how things look to them, or any other possible combination of systems. This tells you that their lead system is different than their representational system. Experientially they access information through one system but bring into consciousness information of another modality.

For instance, a client referred to me after two suicide attempts, expressed feelings of deep depression, hopelessness and so on. Each time I asked him, "How do you know you are depressed" or "What are you feeling hopeless about?" he would access up and left (eidetic visual) and say "I don't know. I just feel it." In this case his lead system was outside of his conscious awareness. As such he truly had no idea what was producing these feelings. By using overlap (pg. 95) I was able to assist him in seeing his internally generated pictures. There was one repetitively occurring image from his past. It was of his wife as he stood next to her hospital bed. She was dying of Hodgkins' Disease and indeed he had felt depressed and hopeless standing by watching her die. Not being aware of what had generated his feelings had left him with few choices to cope with them. Once his visual lead system was brought into his conscious awareness the feelings were known to be a response to a past experience rather than to the present. We worked further using "reframing" (pg. 127) to develop his ability to access pictures which were more useful and productive to his ongoing experience.

Another client complained of feeling worthless, especially in regards to his wife. Each time he mentioned feeling worthless he looked down and left. When asked what he was saying to himself, he said "Nothing, I just feel worthless." Somehow, the feelings of worthlessness were being generated. They did not just arise spontaneously. There was nothing in sensory experience to generate such feelings (his wife wasn't there). The accessing cue would indicate there was internal dialogue outside of his conscious awareness that was generating such feelings. As the session proceeded, this proved to be true. By using the process of overlap (explained in a later section of this book), this client was able to bring the offending voice and message into consciousness (it was his mother's voice repeatedly harping about his being "good for nothing"). Once this was accomplished, the voice could be dealt with directly. The worthless feelings ceased and were replaced by more useful and more satisfying ones.

Another case involved a man suffering from impotence. Each time he described the series of events that constituted his experience of impotency, he would look up and left, and say, "I feel like I can't do it; I feel like I'm bound to fail." Later work revealed that he was accessing an eidetic image of his first experience of impotency, which occurred years earlier. When this picture was accessed, he responded with feelings congruent with that image. But only the feelings were in consciousness. He did not *see* the picture. Once his visual lead system was brought into his conscious awareness, he could generate eidetic pictures of times when he was, in his words, "very studly," and have feelings about himself that were congruent with those pictures which contributed greatly to his sexual experiences.

Problems related to jealousy typically involve a difference between lead and representational systems, with one of these systems occurring outside of consciousness. Often, people feel jealous without knowing the reason for such feelings. In such instances, accessing cues usually indicate a lead system that is outside conscious awareness.

For example, a woman sits home alone waiting for her husband to arrive. She generates internal images of her husband lingering over a conversation with another woman or perhaps an image of him actually intimately involved with another woman. As these images occur, she responds to them with feelings of jealousy. This process is especially out of control if she is not conscious of her own internal imagery. If this is the case, then she knows only that she is experiencing extremely jealous feelings, without knowing from whence they come. As such, she has no choice about the feelings because they come from outside of her conscious awareness and she can't choose to generate other, more useful images which could thus change how she feels. All to often this woman would respond to her husband as though the unseen images had actually occurred.

Such internal process interactions are not at all uncommon. Each of these internal conflicts are examples of how internal processes can be used to impoverish rather than to enrich individual experience. The underlying therapeutic goal in working with such internal conflicts is to make each and every internal process a resource. As a resource each internal process contributes to the fullness of the overall experience either as a stimulus which leads the individual to the desired experience or by adding another complimentary sensory dimension to the experience.

In the case of sexual dysfunction, effective therapy is often a matter of teaching a client to use various externally-generated and/or internally-generated stimuli in all systems, thereby resulting in a pleasurable kinesthetic representation. That is, to use any modality internally or externally to generate desired feelings.

internal

visualizing sexy pictures	feel sexual excitement
internal dialogue describing sexual feelings	feel sexual feelings
remembering kinesthetically the last time you felt highly stimulated sexually	feel sexual stimulation

external

see that partner is aroused	feel aroused
hear partner's aroused breathing	feel aroused
feel touch of partner's body	feel aroused

In summary—besides using your senses to detect a person's representational system and most typical lead system you can also discern which, if any of their internal processes are outside of their conscious awareness. To identify when a lead system is outside of conscious awareness, observe accessing cues and listen to predicates, noting when and if there is an incongruity between the two. If there is, investigate further by asking directly or by employing some more covert means to ascertain if the lead system is indeed outside of consciousness. This information can indicate the best direction to proceed therapeutically as well as establish a basis for judging therapeutic success. Certainly your client's experiential goals are most easily produced when he is facile at manipulating his own internal processes to produce desired experiences for himself and his loved ones.

Neurolinguistic Programming—Internal Strategies

There are even finer distinctions than a person's representational and lead system to be made. These finer distinctions further involve the internal processes and their relationship to external behavior. This is the domain of neurolinguistic programming. The science of subjective experience developed by my colleagues and me. The following are examples of such sequences and interactions of internal processes. I'm sure you will find some of them familiar—as the client who says:

"Well (eyes up, right), it looks like a great opportunity. I can really see myself getting ahead that way. But (eyes down, right), it just feels risky to my marriage. (This illustrates a discrepancy between how the client's visual and kinesthetic systems treat "opportunity.")
Or,
     (Eyes down, left) "It sounds logical enough, but (eyes up, left) I can't see it happening, and that (eyes down, right) makes me feel bad." (Tells himself, but doesn't see eidetic image of it and feels bad about it.)
Or,
     "Well (eyes down, left), I know I shouldn't be promiscuous, but when (eyes up) I see a great-looking guy and I can see he wants me, (eye's down, right) I feel I can't say no." (Tells herself internal dialogue, but visual images determine feelings and therefore in her case external behavior.)
Or,
     "I (eyes up, right) think about all the things I should do to please him and turn him on, but (eyes down, right) I just can't bring myself to do them." (In this case, she thinks in constructed images, but her feelings are too incongruent with her pictures to act on.)

In every case, the accessing cues offer a wealth of information that the words don't provide.

Often, even though persons are flexible as to their lead and representational systems and their internal processes are in their conscious awareness, the specific interactions of various systems produce conflict.

For instance:

     "I don't know why I'm jealous. It's just a feeling (touches midline, eyes down and right). (Eyes down, left) I tell myself there's no reason, but I just think (eyes up and right) of all the things she might be doing and I get jealous (eyes down, right)."

(This example shows how systems often interrelate. He makes constructed images of what she might be doing and feels bad about the pictures even though his internal dialogue says there's no "reason" to. Thus, in this case, his feelings are generated from internal images while his internal dialogue is a polarity response perhaps needing external visual information in order to agree with visual and kinesthetic processes.) Doing therapy with such individuals is quite similar to family therapy as it becomes necessary to resolve differences between internal processes. They are all acting in the person's best interests but do not contain enough similar information to agree upon how those best interests will be served.

People often generate their experience through either simple or sometimes elaborate sequences of internal processes and external behaviors. We refer to these sequences as strategies. For instance, a person might make pictures that generate feelings, then talk about the feelings to himself in words, then picture how someone would look if he knew what he was saying to himself and so on. A past client of mine, a woman, would think of some new technique or sexual enticement she felt would be great to do with her mate. But as she thought about it (made pictures of doing it) she would say to herself that he might say suspiciously "where did you learn that?," and then she would feel hurt and see herself trying to explain without being defensive, and would tell herself that she had better not do the new behavior after all. She used this same "strategy" to inhibit any new behavior. She would imagine herself in a new dress, tell herself her husband would insult her in it, she would feel hurt and defensive and then tell herself she had better not buy it after all. Obviously, it was difficult, to say the least, to persuade this woman to act out new behaviors without changing this strategy.

An aspect of neurolinguistic programming (originated by John Grinder, Richard Bandler, Leslie Cameron Bandler, Judith DeLozier and Robert Dilts) involves understanding and using these more complex interactions of internal and external experience. To give the reader a whisper or glimmer or taste or tickle of what this could mean in therapeutic terms, the following descriptions are offered. In each I have discussed the use of the existing strategies. Another choice would have been to alter the basic strategies themselves. Such a move produces the most pervasive of behavioral and experiential change possible. Too many decision variables are involved in that kind of therapeutic intervention to be mentioned here.

A newly-married couple came in because their love life was not as they hoped it would be. The central aspect of their difficulties was that she did not "feel" wanted or really "feel" loved. This was in spite of his having married her and his many adamant verbalizations that he did indeed love her. During the session, an incident concerning the return and exchange of a wedding present was recounted. They both agreed about returning the gift, but not on what to exchange it for. He offered arguments of value and aesthetics and equal rights: all to no avail. After arguing quite a while, suddenly she very happily gave in to him. This caught my interest so I pursued with her just what had occurred that convinced her to change her position so radically. In her words, "Well (eyes down, left), when I stopped listening to his arguments, which I just couldn't accept (eyes up, left), and just looked at him, I could see how much he really wanted it and I felt like it was important to him. And I just said (eyes down, left) to myself, 'Here is a chance to really make him happy,' and (eyes down, right) that made me feel good, so I gave in to him, and I could see that I really did make him happy."

Thus was revealed to me some pertinent information about how this woman generated her experience. In this context, the information concerned how she became convinced of something. When she "stopped listening" was the first step. Verbally, both internally and externally, she was characteristically full of "yes, buts." So, when she stopped listening and therefore arguing, she *saw* him and the expression on his face was interpreted by her to mean he really wanted it. This generated positive feelings which generated internal dialogue saying she could make him happy, which generated more good feelings and then action. She knew she had done the "right" thing because she could see that he was indeed happy.

Utilizing her strategy, I asked him to make various facial expressions until she could identify which one meant that he loved her and which one meant that he desired her sexually (they turned out to be the same one). Although this seemed an awkward task, they quickly got into the spirit of it. Once the expression was identified, I sent him into the other room with a mirror to practice until he could make that facial expression at will. Meanwhile, I asked her to remember his expression when he looked at her "that" way and then asked what her experience was. Of course, it followed the aforementioned pattern. She saw he wanted her and loved her and this made her feel very loved and important and desirable. She would say to herself, "I can give him what he wants," which generated feelings of arousal for her.

Bringing him back in, I gave them both instructions so that whenever she argued or stated she didn't feel loved and wanted by him, he was to stop talking and she was to stop listening. He was then to tell her, in the only way she could really understand (visually), that he did indeed love and want her, continuing to do so until she responded. Thus, I used her naturally-occurring strategy to achieve a desired therapeutic goal for both of them.

Another couple came for help because of years of tumultuous ups and downs in their relationship. They were both highly visual but manifested the pairing principle[4] within their differing processing strategies. Their verbal labeling of his strategies for generating behavior in the world was "realistic" while hers was "idealistic."

He would become aware of any form of pain which could be either emotional or physical. Then he would see, internally, what this pain kept him from doing. So, his experience went from feeling pain to an image from his past of himself happy without pain and then to internal dialogue suggesting ways of relieving the pain and attaining the feelings in his internal image. At this point, he would make eidetic images of any evidence he had that any of the verbal suggestions would work. If he could see proof that these suggestions would work, he would then act on them. If he couldn't find any proof in his past experience he would decide that nothing could be done about the pain and he would just have to live with it.

This couple's biggest bone of contention was remarrying and again co-parenting their combined seven children. She wanted to remarry and he did not. When he considered marrying her he would feel the pain losing her would bring and then make pictures of himself being happy with her, he would then verbalize suggestions for making this continued happiness come true. But, since the next step was eidetic images—that is, images from the past—and all his past pictures only verified that they could not be happy living together with the children, he didn't act on any of the verbal suggestions and was resigned to staying separated from her. He complained a lot about how she needed to see that being married wouldn't work out; it could only be like before, and she needed to accept that.

He used the same process to generate most of his behavior. For example, he had hated his job for years, but couldn't see how it could be different despite suggestions from all around that he could be a consultant or do freelance work. It was only when he saw that a colleague had done just that and was succeeding very nicely that he believed he could do it, too. Once verified to him that this possibility was indeed viable, he wasted no time in acting on it. All his behavior fit this pattern: future behavior being generated from past experience which was stored in images.

She, on the other hand, began with internal dialogue which told her life could be better, then she generated *constructed* images of possible futures. For each picture, she would have a feeling response. The picture that generated the "best" feeling would be the one she would try to make into reality. Her internal dialogue generated suggestions as to how she could make the picture into reality and she would act on those suggestions. Her behavior would be very direct and straightforward, but if she ran into too many obstacles in making her picture into reality and finally "saw" that she couldn't get to her desired picture, she would feel cheated out of getting what was possible. In the case of their remarrying, she generated pictures of them with their children being happy and loving, and worked towards realizing that. When he resisted, she felt he was cheating her of attaining this happiness. Her behavior was generated from her constructed images which promised the best of all possible futures.

Thus, their strategies led them into conflict, although each was a useful strategy in some ways. His kept him from wasting time and energy *chasing rainbows,* and hers allowed her to frequently attain seemingly impossible goals. Their strategies, however, were also liabilities in some ways. At times, his was limiting and kept him from achieving desired goals because there wasn't a way for him to take any but the most calculated risks. Her strategy frequently led her to disappointment and disillusionment because her desired state was just too far out of reach, especially when she made images that also involved him, which required that he perform some new behaviors to make the image into a reality. Given his strategy, this was often impossible, particularly if the new behaviors had no past experiences from which to be generated.

I chose to work with this couple with a conscious mind orientation. That is, I explicitly displayed to their conscious minds their own and each other's strategies. Once understood, I demonstrated to them how their conflicts were a result of their strategies and little else. Then I taught them how to use one another's strategies for more successful communication. He learned how to give her descriptions of "more realistic" pictures that were more easily attainable but which also generated very positive feelings for her. For instance, she would make pictures of what great fun they would have doing outdoor athletic things together. This was fine except that he suffered from a very bad back. He would just say no, it was impossible, and she would knock herself out trying to get him to enjoy athletic outings. When he didn't, she felt bad and resented him for being such a "stick in the mud." In her words, "If I had a bad back, I'd do anything to make it better. I'd try anything and everything; but not him. He'd rather keep his bad back." Of course, he only pursued remedies for which he had seen absolute proof. And since he did not search out evidence for all the suggested remedies, he really did very little about it. To work on this issue, I had him describe various scenes to her in which the two of them were very happy together in quiet, serene surroundings, engaged in activities better suited and more comfortable for his back condition. She then chose the one which *felt* best to her. Thus, he learned to use her strategy to generate a desirable, yet more "realistic" and achievable outcome for the two of them. Meanwhile, I instructed her to offer no suggestions to him concerning possible alternatives or remedies unless she also provided substantial evidence to verify the value of her suggestions.

In another context, she wished him to open up communication channels between himself and her daughter. His past experience led him to believe this would be foolhardy at best. I persuaded her to stop frustrating herself with suggesting to him what to do and instead use her energies to create an experience between him and her daughter in which *any* form of communication would be seen as productive by him. Once such an experience had occurred, his future behavior could meet her desires. In these ways, therefore, they were able both to understand their processes of relating and, when the need arose, to utilize them to bypass conflicts, thereby enhancing their experience.

In these cases you can see how a rigid sequence of internal

processes influences a person's behavior. Like these people we are all subject to the experiences and behaviors our strategies lead us to. Since strategies are composed of rigid sequences of internal processes the more facile each of us is at manipulating these processes the greater our ability to construct one which leads us to the experiences and behaviors we desire.

Utilizing Representational Systems and Accessing Cues To Establish Rapport

In the previous section, you learned how to identify representational systems and accessing cues. There are, of course, nonverbal behaviors other than accessing cues that can also be used to identify specific internal processes. These include voice tone shifts, skin temperature fluctuations, changes in facial color and muscle tone, and variations in breathing patterns. Any of these can provide similar information about internal processing. I encourage you to investigate these patterns of sensory experience on your own.

Matching

Building on the foundation already provided, this section deals with how representational systems and accessing cues can be powerfully utilized in the process of change. To effectively gather information or begin a process of change it will always be important to establish rapport between yourself and your client at both the conscious and unconscious level. An invaluable technique for doing just this is to generate verbal and nonverbal behavior which matches that of your client. This is called "matching". The client's subjective experience becomes one of being really understood. After al¹, you are speaking their language verbally and nonverbally.

The process of matching representational system and accessing cues requires that the therapist: (1) be able to recognize what representational system and accessing cues the client is operating from; (2) be flexible enough in his own behavior to communicate in the language of any representational system and to direct his own eye movements at will; and (3), in order to accomplish the above, be able to keep his own consciousness attentive to sensory experience rather than accessing internally himself. Because of the trade-off between internal and external experience, if the therapists's consciousness is on internally-accessed experience, he will be missing the verbal and nonverbal communications offered by the client. It is appalling to notice therapists conducting sessions with their eyes closed. For successful intervention, the therapist must be alert to sensory experience.

The following examples of matching will serve to clarify this task:

(1) June: "Well (eyes up, left), it's clear to me he isn't interested
              in changing what's going on."
    Ther: "Oh? The way you see it (eyes up, left) your husband
              is satisfied with what is happening now."
    June: "He must be. I can't (eyes up, left; head shakes no)
              invision him being any different, either."
    Ther: "So you don't have (eyes left) a picture yet of how
              you'd like him to be? (Eyes up, right) Imagine that." (Thera-
              pist leads client with non verbal behavior of constructed
              image accessing cue which is congruent with imagining a
              picture June has never seen before.

(2) Meg: "He just doesn't see who I am."
    Ther: "Oh, who does he see you as?"
    Meg: "I don't know; I just know it isn't me."
    Ther: "How will you *show* him the real you so he can take a
              look?" (This asks the client to begin eliciting the response
              she wants with her own behavior)

(3) Joe: "Listen (eyes down, left), there is nothing but discord in
              our relationship, and everything I've ever tried to do has
              only amplified (eyes down, left) our problem."
    Ther: "Hmmm, if I hear you right, then you would like things
              to quiet down and perhaps have some harmony develop
              between the two of you."
    Joe: "Yeah, now you're tuned in to what I want."

(4) Shirley: "If I could just feel like he was trying. But he just
              turns away, pulls the covers over his head, anything but face
              up to what's going on."
    Ther: "If I grasp what you're saying, then you feel like he is
              out of touch with what's going on and you have to knock him
              over to get his attention."

In instances where unspecified predicates are used, the accessing cue can indicate how the therapist may effectively structure
these communications in such a way as to pace the client:

(1) Betsy: "I want you to know that she (up, left) really tried. I
              don't think (down, left) there is anything more to do."
    Ther: "So, you see what already has been done and you tell
              yourself there isn't anything left?"

(2) Jimmy: (Down, right) "There isn't anything left here for me. It's a disaster."

Ther: "You feel like there isn't anything to hold onto and perhaps nothing that can or will hold onto you."

(3) Sam: "We would be (eyes up, right) okay if there was more respect around here."

Ther: "What do you see yourself doing that would show your wife how much you respect her?" (referential index shift— He wants respect—How does he express respect to others)

(4) Theresa: "Well, just when (down, left) we're getting along, something happens and *bang* (up, left) we're at it again."

Ther: "Sounds (down, left) to me like just when you tell yourself it's okay, bang (up left) and you can see trouble happening all over again."

Translating

Besides matching predicates and accessing cues, when therapy involves more than one person the therapist must bridge the communications gap which exists between the clients. This task requires that the therapist be able to translate in experiential terms from one representational system to another.

For instance, to some highly visual people the experience of living in a very messy, untidy house is comparable to the experience of sleeping in a bed full of cracker crumbs for a highly kinesthetic person. Or, for a kinesthetic person being pushed away is like being left out of the picture would be for a visual person. For the auditory-digital person, being illogical could be the equivalent of an unpleasant rockoplane ride for the kino or a psychedelic light show for the visual. To think in terms of translating experience from one modality into another requires the therapist be able to represent various experiences in any modality. For instance, the auditory experience of silence could be likened to the kinesthetic experience of numbness and the visual experience of total darkness. Or, the visual process of imagining could translate as a process of constructing for a kino or a process of orchestrating for an auditory person. All of these are brief illustrations of experiential translations. Following are two examples taken from therapy transcripts which serve to demonstrate this process in a therapeutic context.

"Transcript A"

Joseph: (Eyes up, left) "Well, I think our difficulty is different from most people."

Ther: "Oh, how do you see it?"

Jo: "Well, she is the impatient one (up, left). I like to plan how it will be. You know, set the stage."

Ther: "How do you plan?"

Jo: (Eyes up, right) "Well. . . ."

Th: "I understand. So you enjoy picturing what will take place."

Jo: "Yes. I really get off on planning and changing the plans until it's just perfect, then I like to live out those fantasies. And they all have Janis in them. I want you to know that."

Th: "So, let me see if I understand you (eyes up, left; gestures with hands up in front of eyes), you create a visual fantasy of you and Janis making love from beginning to end, an elaborate and detailed fantasy. And when it looks right to you, then you want to make that fantasy into reality by having the two of you act it out. Is that right?"

Jo: "Yes."

Ther: "Okay, now I'm going to ask Janis some questions and I want you to watch closely." "Janis (therapist reaches over and touches her lightly on her left arm), and what do you feel you want?"

Janis: "Well (eyes down, right; then left), I just feel like all that is so silly. I don't want to be part of a play. I want to feel wanted without all the buildup. It doesn't have any spontaneity."

Joseph: "See, she just isn't very romantic!"

Janis: "And you're not very spontaneous either!"

Th: "Whoa! Wait a minute" (holds Janis's arm, puts hand in "stop" gesture in front of Joe's face). "Now, Janis, suppose you tell me what you do want instead of what you don't want. Can you get in touch with how you'd like it to be? And you watch closely, Joe."

Ja: (Eyes down, right) "I just want it to be more fun. I'd like him to let me surprise him; but no, it's always according to plan. And the lighting has to be just right and the soft music playing. I want to just grab him sometimes, you know. When I feel like having sex, I want it right then."

Th: "I think I can grasp what you are saying. You feel like you would be happier if when you felt the urge to have sex with Joe you could reach for him or let him know and he would respond. You would like to feel like there could be more surprises."

Ja: "Yes, that's it. Surprises."

Th: "Now, Joe, I want you to pay close attention because I'm going to show Janis what you want in a way I think will make sense to her. Okay?"

Jo: "Okay. This ought to be good."

Th: "Janis, have you ever prepared a four or five course meal?"

Ja: "Well, yes, a couple of times."

Th: "And have you had the pleasure of enjoying having a four or five course meal served to you?"

Ja: "Yes."

Th: "And each course was well planned and designed to whet your appetite for the next. . . . correct?"

Ja: "Well, yes."

Th: "When you prepared such a meal, would you have felt disappointed if your guests had put all five courses on the table at once and just dived in, or worse yet if before you started serving they satisted themselves on a leftover tuna fish sandwich?"

Ja: (Laughing) "Well, yes. Yes, I'd feel disappointed, even mad."

Th: "Well, that's something like what happens to Joseph. He makes plans that are intended to delight you and take you exciting places, and he gets disappointed if you founder yourself on the appetizer."

Ja: "But—"

Th: "Before you "but" I want to know if you can be in touch with how that would be for him."

Ja: (Nods head up and down.)

Th: "Good. Now, I'm going to let Joseph in on how it is for you. So, hold on there for a moment." "Joseph, have you ever taken a tour with a tour guide . . . as a student or something like that?"

Jo: "Only once, in Hawaii."

Th: "Well, on that tour the guide had a very specific itinerary drawn out. And probably you pictured beforehand some of what you would see."

Jo: "Yeah."

Th: "While you were on this tour, if you looked this way or that, you may have seen a fascinating side road or curio shop. And you wanted a closer look. But, alas, it was not included on the tour and the opportunity to explore that unexpected object of interest just disappeared as your tour guide directed your attention back to the planned itinerary. Can you see how frustrating that would be? It could even lead to your being disillusioned with going on such tours, don't you think?"

Jo: "Well. . . . you mean, I'm being like a tour director?"

Ja: "Yes. Yes, you are."

Th: "Of course, sometimes being taken on a tour can be a very delicious experience like being served an eight course meal. And other times, exploring a new avenue on the spur of the moment can be thrilling. Don't you agree?"

"Transcript B"

Th: "Tell me what you would like to be different in this relationship."

Ron: (Frown's eyes down-left, down-right) "Well, I think it would help if there was more (eyes down, right) cooperation."

Th: "And what could your wife Sue Ann do that would help you to *feel* like there was cooperation?"

R: "Oh, if she'd just understand that I work hard and sometimes the pressure gets to me, you know? It's rough going at work and I come home and she just piles more on."

Th: "So, you feel like she adds to the burden and what you'd like is for her to lend a hand and lighten the load. Is that right?"

R: "That's about it. Yeah."

Th: "Well, you hold on for a moment, Ron, while I talk to Sue Ann. "Sue Ann, I'm sure you want to reply to what Ron just said, but first I want you to tell me what you want to be different."

Sue Ann: (Eyes up, left) "It doesn't matter."

Th: (Eyes up, left) "What doesn't matter?"

S: (Eyes up, left) "What I want, that's what. Nothing's going to change. Never has, never will."

Th: "You don't like what you see going on now, right?" (Eyes lead Sue Ann's up and left.)

S: "That's right."

Th: "Well, if you could take that picture you have of what's going on with you and Ron and change it . . . what would you change in that picture so it would look better to you?"

S: "Well, I'd like to see that he appreciates me. Oh, shit! Look at him. What's the use? Everytime I think, "Oh, maybe things could be better," but it's just one disillusionment after another. If I think it's gonna get brighter, sure enough—"click"—it's lights out and I wanna tell you it's dark as hell."

Th: "Let me see if I understand. The picture I have is that you get your hopes up, you imagine how good it could be and— "click"—something happens that makes those hopes disappear. Right?"

S: "Yeah."

Th: "Sue Ann, I want you to watch closely and see if I can get Ron to see a little of your point of view, okay?"

S: "Okay."

Th: "Ron, what Sue Ann would like you to be in touch with is how disappointed she gets sometimes. Have you ever built a sand castle on the shoreline as the tide came in; and even though you really worked hard to keep that castle standing, the tide would come in and knock it down? Until finally, you quit trying to build or rebuild the sand castle. It just seems like too much for you to handle alone. That's what Sue Ann feels happens to her hopes. They get built up only to be knocked down. So, now she pretty much doesn't hope."

R: "I never meant to knock down her hopes."

Th: "I believe you. While you think a bit about that, I'm going to talk to Sue Ann about what you want."

Th: "Sue Ann, let me see if I can give you a picture of Ron's request. Have you ever been away from home, come home and found the house a mess? As you looked around and saw all the things that needed to be done, it seemed an overwhelming and very gloomy task and, worst of all, there was no help in sight. Well, I think that's how it looks sometimes to Ron."

"Now, each of you are here to obtain help from me in order to relate to each other better. And I agree that you need that help. But, what neither of you has been aware of is how much the other one needs you. How much Sue Ann needs your help in building hopes and dreams that come true and how much Ron needs your help to clear the path so he can see what there is to hope and dream about. Each of you has perhaps thought that if the other won, you would lose. But not so. If either of you wins, you both win but if either of you loses, you both lose."

In these two examples, I matched predicates and accessing cues in order to build trust and rapport, translated each client's position to the other in experiential terms, and used unspecified predicates to talk with both of them at once. These methods of use, though simple, are of a very useful nature.

Identifying the Dysfunctional Context

Thus far I have presented to you information about how to
detect the client's representational systems and accessing cues and
how to use them for establishing rapport. Now I would like to turn
your skills towards learning the systemic nature of the client's
sexual dysfunction. While identifying a client's most typical representational system, lead system, and establishing rapport provides
the therapist with a wealth of vital information, it is not really
sufficient for successful therapy.

As previously stated, human experience is made up of interactions between external stimuli and internal processes. In
order to understand the process of dysfunction that an individual or couple is suffering from, it is necessary to identify the
various experiential elements which constitute the dysfunctional
context. Indeed, the field of family therapy originated as a result of this necessity. Psychotherapists noticed that schizo-
phrenics who had been cured often resumed their symptomatic
behavior when placed back in their families. Further investigation proved that certain behaviors on the part of family members triggered the identified patient back into schizophrenia.
Even in less severely disturbed cases, it has almost always been
found that any such symptomatic behavior makes sense when
considered within the family context.

If you have worked with runaway teenagers I'm sure your experience verifies this concept. So often parents find their teenagers
behavior incomprehensible while to the therapist viewing the family from a different perspective the motivations for rebellious behavior are so often obvious.

I remember a case from years back which bears this in mind.
A young girl fifteen had been absent from her highschool for
over two weeks. She was attending a special alternative highschool for youths who had been in trouble at their previous
highschool and with the law. It was a very progressive school
with an enrollment of only forty students with three staff members. This girl had always loved this school and was at the time
living in the best foster placement available so her behavior was
peculiar in the least. I had clients who attended this school and
the staff asked me to look into this situation. It was a serious
one for if the staff reported her truancy she would be placed

.h the California Youth Authority once again. I found the girl
...ding out at a friend's place. She was at first completely silent
and answered my questions with shrugs. With the help of her
friend I was able to slowly draw the needed answers from her.
It turned out that her behavior stemmed from shyness rather
than rebellion. Each morning and afternoon a group meeting
of students and staff took place at school. Its purpose was to
air grievances, express appreciation and generally to reinforce
positive social behaviors. This particular girl rarely if ever
spoke during these meetings. As a result a staff member had
taken her aside and told her she would not be able to stay in
the school if she did not contribute to the group by speaking
and sharing of herself. This was done with the best of intentions but it backfired completely. Rather than overcome her
shyness (which she often disguised with sullen shrugs) she
stopped going to school altogether. She had rationalized that
they would soon expell her anyway.

This example shows how the girl's behavior makes sense when
the larger social context is understood. Usually the behaviors triggering unwanted experiences in a couple or a family are far more
subtle. Perhaps you have had the experience of working with a
couple when suddenly they are deep into an argument which is
incomprehensible to you as to what it is about and how it began.
It may have been that only with a careful dissection of their respec-
tive behaviors did you learn how each time he sighed in a certain
way she immediately became terribly angry.

I remember seeing a couple whose problems stemmed from
just such a subtle but persistent aspect of the husband's behavior. There was very little successful communication between the
couple and they had not had sexual relations for about seven
years. As I worked with them it became apparent that she was
highly visual while he was primarily kinesthetic. Although this
produced some of their communication problems, the crux of
their difficulties was occuring at a more subtle level of behavior.
Each time she moved her head and eyes up and to the left in
order to access visually, he would look down and right accessing
kinesthetically. As he did this, he had the habit of sucking on his
lips, producing a clicking sound similar to the sound a slide pro-
jector makes as it changes slides. Interestingly, it is just such a
sound that consistently changes a person's internally-generated

pictures. If you make an image and then make a "clicking" noise with tongue against the back of the top teeth, typically the image disappears. Certainly this is what happened to his wife as she accessed visually and her husband sucked his lips. Each time this occurred, she became understandably frustrated and furious. For her, it was impossible to even think around him. It is important to note that neither of them understood the significance of his "clicking" noise in this process. Thus, each time he "clicked" her thinking process was interrupted, to which she responded with anger. He then became perplexed and felt genuinely abused by her behavior towards him. This is an example of how an external stimuli (his clicking) triggered an interaction that exemplified their dysfunctional system. This particular sequence of external and internal processes occurred each time she accessed visually for more than a second or two; and, being highly visual, she did so frequently. I learned that they had remained together over the years due to communications that had occurred either by letter or telephone conversation, this made sense since both of these communication mediums made it impossible to trigger the problematic behavior.

In this case my knowledge of accessing cues and internal processes proved invaluable in determining what triggered this couple's problematic behavior. It is possible to think of such a trigger as the stimulus or cause and the resultant behaviors as the response or effect. As such I would like to undertake a discussion of just how stimulus-response or cause effect behaviors relate to an understanding of the clients' sexual dysfunction.

Stimulus-Response

Phobias are really explicit examples of how some external stimulus trigger internal processes which result in an undersirable experience. For example, a person may look down from a height and feel herself falling and be overcome with terror. It's not just the looking down which frightens her, but also the feeling of falling that looking down triggers. A woman came to me because of her phobic response to having sexual intercourse in the classic missionary position (which happened to be the position preferred by her husband). Whenever he lay on top of her, she went into a panicky rage, screaming and kicking. No amount of conscious desire on her part could alter this sequence of events. The possible causes of this response were outside of conscious awareness for her as were any internal processes that occurred in the given context. There was only the weight on her chest and abdomen and the next thing she knew she had thrown her husband off and was panting and sweating from fear and exertion. By taking her back in time, we learned that her older siblings had once wrestled her to the floor, sat upon her, and then put a pillow over her face to stifle her screams. To her, this became a life or death struggle. Long forgotten, it was only in the sexual context that she experienced a similar heavy weight on her body. When this occurred, it triggered unconscious processes that associated such weight with the previous life or death struggle.

Phobias can be triggered by an internally-generated image, sound, or feeling which, when experienced externally, produces the phobic response as well. For the person who is phobic of snakes, for example, thinking about touching a snake will produce much the same response as being presented with an actual snake. People can produce within themselves, with very little corroboration from external experience, emotional states that they may or may not want. What is important is knowing *how* they elicit such a response from themselves. Similarly, knowing how the behavior of one member of a couples elicits certain responses from his/her partner is important to understanding how their experiences as a couple are produced.

The Meta Model (Appendix I) contains a linguistic method for gathering information about a client's *verbally* expressed stimulus-response or cause and effect behaviors. To quote from *The Structure Of Magic I*:

Cause and Effect

This class of semantically ill-formed Surface Structures involves the belief on the part of the speaker that one person (or set of circumstances) may perform some action which necessarily causes some other person to experience some emotion or inner state. Typically, the person experiencing this emotion or inner state is portrayed as having no choice in responding the way he does. For example, the client says,

. . . .*My wife makes me feel angry.*

Notice that this Surface Structure presents a vague image in which one human being (identified as *My wife*) performs some action (unspecified) which necessarily causes some other person (identified as *me*) to experience some emotion *(anger)*. Ill-formed Surface Structures which are members of this class can be identified by one of two general forms:

(A)   X Verb   Y Verb   Adjective
      (cause)   (feel experience)   (some emotion or
                                              some inner state)

Thus Bandler and Grinder find it useful to challenge cause and effect. I agree. It is important to note, however, that the existence of such stimulus-response/cause-effect phenomena is not denied by the linguistic challenges. Rather ill-formedness occurs when a person experiences *only one* possible response or effect to a stimulus. This is where the distortion occurs. (Not that a wife's behavior has an effect on her husband, but that he would *have* to respond only in anger to her behavior.) That Bandler and Grinder make this distinction and even use the processes to influence their own and other's experience is apparent both in their own behavior and in their ensuing publications, especially Patterns II and Neurolinguistic Programming I.

Although clients bring in many different kinds of problems, worries, woes, hopes and dreams, the effective therapist changes the same aspect of each of them. That is, the therapist does not change the stimulus the world provides the client so much as he or she changes how the client responds to that stimulus. Even if the therapist assists the client in changing jobs, locales, spouses, schools, etc., if the client does not respond to his new environment in more useful ways, the patterns that brought him into therapy will be repeated. This is especially evident in the area of sexual dysfunction where, so often, changing sexual partners does not alter the dysfunctional sexual behavior.

The problems clients bring in are examples of how they respond to the stimuli around them. Indeed, that they have come to therapy is a statement that they would like to have a different response or experience, at least with regard to some aspect of that stimuli. Often a new response to an old stimulus can generate such pervasive change that a person's whole life experience is much improved.

It might seem to many that accepting cause and effect or stimulus-response is starting out already defeated. It's true we must respond to the stimulus, and usually that response is operative at the unconscious level. Also, that response is often predetermined by learnings that took place early in our development when we did not have the faculties to question them. On the face of it, that does seem to leave us helpless. Certainly, these very thoughts have kept humanistic psychology people at odds with behaviorists for years. It makes us seem so like rats in a maze.

However, I use two crucial differences; namely, (1) we can change how we respond to most stimuli, and (2) possibly the most important difference is that we can acquire several choices for responding and then choose the one most appropriate for generating the desired results in a specific context.

Most human behavior dealt with in the therapeutic context is learned. Straight stimulus-response theory is based primarily upon responses that are "wired" into us as a species. Examples of these are: Loud noise—startle reflex. Presentation of food after abstinence—salivation. Quick movements around eyes—blink reflex. But more important for our purpose are those *learned* responses which are then generated at the unconscious level in response to specific stimuli.

In this culture, the handshake is an example of a learned response which then occurs at the unconscious level. In fact, if the sequence of behaviors leading to the completion of a handshake is interrupted, the person involved may enter a quite altered state of consciousness (see Bandler, Grinder, and DeLozier, *Patterns II*). Try it yourself: The next time someone extends their hand to you for the customary handshake, try not to respond. Doubtless, you will find it difficult indeed. Answering a ringing telephone is another learned response and yet difficult to override. Notice how the conscious mind makes the distinction concerning whether or not the phone is yours. If it isn't, often the stimulus-response pattern is thereby interrupted.

The process of understanding language is also a phenomenon of learned stimulus-response. Words do not have meaning in and of themselves any more than a completely unfamiliar language carries meaning for us. Language is comprised of specific sounds organized in a sequence with specific intonation patterns. These certain sequences of sounds and intonation patterns become meaningful when they are associated with some specific sensory experience. The small child is presented with the phenomenon of a dog and as he sees, hears, touches, and smells it, he is also presented with the sounds that make up the word "dog." This process continues to occur and the two associated aspects become so profoundly linked that it becomes nearly impossible to say the word "dog" and not also think of a dog. Thus, we can generously say, "I'll give you the pot of gold at the end of the rainbow if you don't think of a big white duck."

Likewise, the child learns to associate sequences of sounds with the lack of certain sensory experiences—"quiet," for example. Words like comfort, curiosity, interest, sad, and happy become associated with certain inner states. This occurs much like the sound of the ringing bell became associated with food for Pavlov's dogs. The bell came to represent the stimulus of food effectively enough to elicit the salivating response previously only associated with the presentation of food. Since language is meaningful only by its association to sensory experience, the process of understanding language takes place when the sounds trigger an internal response generating some aspect or aspects of the associated sensory experience.

Similarly, as a child you learned to associate specific aspects of your family's behaviors with meanings and learned to respond appropriately. The tone of your mother's voice, the expression on your father's face, the way a door was closed—all came to influence your subsequent behavior. Can you remember how your mother looked and sounded when she was angry? When she was frightened? When she was proud? As you remembered, did you notice how your own experience changed?

It is possible to learn how to *not* respond to our environmental stimuli. We label such behavior as pathological, calling it catatonia or autism, and, certainly, it is unusual to display no outward evidence of responding to the world around us. Even in the most severe cases of catatonia and autism it has been shown that this condition can be altered once the appropriate stimulus is found. That is, there is some stimulus, some behavior on the part of staff or therapist, which can elicit responses, though finding it can often tax both the therapist's creativity and sense of morality (see Farreley, *Provocative Therapy*).

I consider it to be true that the response chosen by any individual to a given stimulus is the best they have available to them, at least in its first occurrence. Richard Bandler and John Grinder expand on this belief in *The Structure of Magic,* volume I:

> Our experience has been that, when people come to us in therapy, they typically come with pain, feeling themselves paralyzed, experiencing no choices or freedom of action in their lives. What we have found is not that the world is too limited or that there are no choices, but that these people block themselves from seeing those options and possibilities that are open to them since they are not available in their models of their world.
>
> Almost every human being in our culture in his life cycle has a number of periods of change and transition which he must negotiate. Different forms of psychotherapy have developed various categories for these important transition-crisis points. What's peculiar is that some people are able to negotiate these periods of change with little difficulty, experiencing these periods as times of intense energy and creativity. Other people, faced with the same challenges, experience these periods as times of dread and pain—periods to be endured, when their primary concern is simple survival. The difference between these two groups appears to us to be primarily that the people who respond creatively to and cope effectively with this stress are people who have a rich representation or model of their situation, one in which they perceive a wide range of options in choosing their actions. The other people experience themselves as having few options, none of which are attractive to them—the "natural loser" game. The question for us is: How is it possible for different human beings faced with the same world to have such different experiences? Our understanding is that this difference follows primarily from differences in the richness of their models. Thus, the question becomes: How is it possible for human beings to maintain an impoverished model which causes them pain in the face of a multivalued, rich, and complex world?
>
> In coming to understand how it is that some people continue to cause themselves pain and anguish, it has been important for us to realize that they are not bad, crazy, or sick. They are, in fact, making the best choices available in their own particular model. In other words, human beings' behavior, no matter how bizarre it may first appear to be, makes sense when it is seen in the context of the choices generated by their model. The diffi-

culty is not that they are making the wrong choice, but that they do not have enough choices.

People can add new, more useful, choices of responding to almost any stimuli. In fact, they can learn any number of responses to a given stimulus and , as a result, be able to choose among them for the one most appropriate. This is precisely what occurs as people grow and change emotionally, enriching the interpersonal aspects of their lives.

Very often rigid response patterns are a result of early learning. Certain stimuli send us back to a childhood state where our adult resources are unavailable. The following example is often used to demonstrate this phenomenon in training workshops. As children, most of us learned to respond with varying degrees of fear to harsh, loud voices, stern faces, and pointed fingers. Most of us learned that such a display was meant to threaten inpending physical punishment and, at the very least, was a vivid display of anger. As children, emotional and physical well being was at stake or was at least believed to be at stake. Even some of the most competent adults still respond to a congruent display such as this with fearfulness. And, even when they know that such a display is only for purposes of demonstration, the response still occurs, being generated at the unconscious level.

So, stimulus X elicits response Y.

And, each time X occurs, it triggers Y.

Staged graphically:

$$X \rightarrow Y$$

This common behavioral pattern shows how a specific stimuli can induce an experiential state where choices are very limited. It is rare that a loud verbal display need cause fear in an adult. Rather any number of responses could be more useful. Listening to what is being said, remaining calm, shouting back, whistling, and so on. There are a number of methods which will be presented to accomplish the relearning process such that a stimulus triggers a choice point rather than an automatic response.

Stimulus X generates the possibilities of responses A, C, M, N, Y, Z when

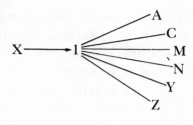

1 Being a choice point

An example in the realm of sexual dysfunction can serve to clarify this concept. Mary was twenty-two years old and sought therapy because, though she desired to, she was unable to have sexual relations with her fiance. The cause of her dysfunction was traced back to an incident that had occurred in her early teens. Her uncle had sexually abused her. In itself, this was not enough to produce a sexual dysfunction, but all the terror, pain and guilt that Mary felt in the past episode had become associated with the picture or sight of an erect penis. So, when Mary saw an erect penis she responded with feelings of terror and revulsion. She and her fiance had attempted to overcome the response by initiating sexual relations in complete darkness. However, as soon as Mary felt an erect penis, she then generated an internal image of it and was therefore triggered into the unwanted response.

So, where X is the stimulus: visual image of erect penis
    (either internally-or externally-generated)
Y is the terror response which results from the past experience.
    Every time X occurs, Y results.
        $$X \longrightarrow Y$$
        This is not at all an unusual phenomenon. Most of us are triggered into past memories by present stimuli. The smell of our first lover's cologne or perfume, or the sound of a record album listened to in the past, can flood us with memories as well as the feelings congruent with those memories. Like so many of our human processes, this one can enhance our experience at times, yet can severely impoverish it at others.

With Mary, the feelings triggered by the visual image of an erect penis were certainly appropriate to the experience that had occurred when she was thirteen, but they were not appropriate to sexual experiences with her fiance; yet, she could not consciously control them. Similarly, the response to harsh shouting and a pointing finger is also an instance of feelings being triggered that belong to the past and are not appropriate for the present. Though fear is certainly a useful response when it is crucial to a warning of danger, it can also be a response that limits a person's ability to operate effectively in the world when triggered unnecessarily or inappropriately. Experiences that may terrify a child, and usually rightfully so, need not bother the adult who, hopefully, has acquired resources to deal with the world that the child cannot know even exist.

Successful intervention in these cases requires interrupting the pattern of X triggering Y and diverting the response to a choice point where the client can choose a more satisfying response (at the unconscious level)

Thus in the past: X ⎯⎯⎯⎯→ Y
                           triggered

The therapist intervenes to create a choice point for the client

             X ⎯⎯⎯⎯⎯⎯⎯⎯⎯⎯→ C
                    triggers choice point C

  C inturn can trigger multiple responses

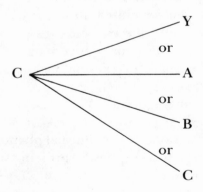

New choices of responding are developed from which the client can choose.

These new choices must, of course, be activated by stimulis response as automatically as was Y.

The old response is kept as a *choice.* Being based upon a powerful past learning it is possible that response would be useful at some future time. I believe all responses are useful at some time, in some context. Once the new learning has been integrated into the client's behavior the need for the therapeutic intervention drops out.

In the case of Mary, I used a meta-technique referred to as a visual-kinesthetic three-placed disassociation. (This technique will be presented in detail in a later section of this work.) It resulted in the subject (Mary) being able to maintain feelings congruent with her present experience (in this case, calm and comfortable) while recalling vividly the past memory. Feelings that are specific to the remembered experience become disassociated while recalling vividly the past memory. *Feelings* that are specific to the remembered experience become disassociated while the subject can still *visualize* the memory. Thus, for Mary, the terror and revulsion became part of the picture and she could have other feelings more appropriate to her current experience. This left Mary's response to the sight of an erect penis open to new possibilities. At this point, Mary's fiance—a very tender, loving young man—was also given instructions designed to help gently guide the two of them toward establishing positive associations for Mary with the naturally-occurring sexual stimuli. And they succeeded beautifully.

Masters and Johnson, too, are certainly familiar with the phenomenon of one intense experience influencing all subsequent similar experiences:

> "Frequently, one particular event, one specifically traumatic episode, has been quite sufficient to terminate the individual male's ability to, facility for, interest in, or demand for ejaculating intravaginally. Occasionally a man may lose ejaculatory facility subsequent to a physically traumatic episode, but usually the only trauma is psychological.
>
> The interesting observation remains that, although there obviously are instances when primary impotence almost seems preordained by prior environmental influence, there frequently is a psychosexually traumatic episode directly associated with the first coital experience that establishes a negative psychosocial influence pattern or even a lifestyle of sexual dysfunction for the traumatized male."[9]

(Masters and Johnson, however, do not outline specific techniques for working with such cases.)

So, where some stimulus triggers an undesirable response, the therapist's task is first to identify this process and then interrupt it in such a way that some new, more useful response or choice of responses results. The meta-techniques of change are especially effective in this process. In order to further clarify this important aspect of stimulus-response, the following case histories recorded by Masters and Johnson of clients who fit these patterns are included in this section.

#1

There are four recorded histories . . . of men with basically stable family, religious, and personal backgrounds whose initial failure at coital connection was specifically associated with a traumatic experience developing from prostitute involvement with their first experience at coition. Three of these virginal young men (two late teenage and one 22-year-old) each sought prostitute opportunity in the most debilitated sections of cities in which they were living and were so repulsed by their neophyte observations of the squalor of the prostitute's quarters, the dehumanizing quality of her approach, and the physically unappetizing, essentially repulsive quality of the woman involved that they could not achieve or maintain an erection. The fact that their own poor judgment had rendered them vulnerable to a level of social environment to which they were unaccustomed and for which they were unprepared never occurred to them. In two of these instances their frantic attempts to extablish an erection amused the prostitutes and their obvious fears of performance were derided. The third young man was assured that "he would never be able to get the job done for any woman—if he couldn't get it done here and now with a pro."

#2

The following history exemplifies onset of vaginismus subsequent to episodes of psychosexual trauma. There have been three women referred to therapy so physically and emotionally traumatized by unwelcome sexual attack that vaginismus developed subsequent to their traumatic experiences.

When first seen, couple C had been married for 18 months, with repeated attempts to consummate the marriage reported as unsuccessful. The husband, age 31, reported effective sexual function with several other women prior to marriage. The wife, age 28, described successful sexual connection with four men over a five-year period before the specific episode of sexual trauma. One of these relationships included coitus two or three times a week over a 10 month time span. She had been readily orgasmic in the association.

The traumatic episode in her history was a well-authenticated episode of gang rape with resultant physical trauma to the victim requiring two week's hospitalization. Extensive surgical reconstruction of the vaginal canal was necessary for basic physical rehabilitation. No psychotherapeutic support was sought by or suggested for the girl following this experience.

Mr. and Mrs. C met one year after the rape episode and were married a year after their introduction. Prior to the marriage the husband-to-be- was in full possession of the factual history of the gang raping and of the resultant physical distress.

During the latter stages of their engagement period, several attempts at intercourse proved unsuccessful in that despite full erection, penetration could not be accomplished. It was mutually agreed that in all probability the security of the marital state would release her presumed hysterical inhibitions. This did not happen. After the marriage ceremony, attempts at consummation continued unsuccessful despite an unusually high degree of finesse, kindness, and discretion in the husband's sexual approaches to his traumatized partner. Severe vaginismus was demonstrated during physical examination of the wife after referral to the Foundation.

#3

The remaining two rape experiences were family-oriented and almost identical in history. In both instances young girls were physically forced by male members of their immediate family to provide sexual release, on numerous occasions, for men they did not know. In one instance, a father, and in another, an older brother, forced sexual partners upon teenage girls (15 and 17 years of age) and repeatedly stood by to insure the girls' physical cooperation. Sexually exploited, emotionally traumatized, and occasionally physically punished, these girls became conditioned to the concept that "all men were like that." When released from family sexual servitude each girl avoided any possibility of sexual contact during the late teens and well into the twenties, until married at 25 and 29 years of age. Even then, they could not make themselves physically available to consummate their marriages, regardless of how strongly they willed sexual cooperation. Severe vaginismus was present in both cases.

Present State and Desired State

I believe sexual functioning to be a sequence of naturally-occurring and interrelated stimulus-response patterns. Masters and Johnson have presented a profound and detailed clinical description of the sequence of physiological responses in both men and women and how they interrelate to one another. Sexual dysfunction occurs when some normal stimulus elicits a response from either partner which is opposed to or incongruent to the naturally-occurring sequence. Often, the therapist need not be terribly concerned with gathering information about the desired state since it is so often obvious in the case of sexual dysfunction. It is rather the present state which somehow prevents the occurrence of the natural sequence of sexual stimulus-response. The therapist's task is one of removing the block in the present state so the desired state can occur.

The problem is not just the present state, but also the organization of internal and external behaviors and responses that generate what is experienced as a problem. This is not so simple a process as asking, "What's wrong?" and "How do you want it to be?" Learning what the client's internal and external behaviors and responses are and the relationships between them requires the ability to make sophisticated distinctions in the area of human behavior. These distinctions are made by further training your ears and eyes to identify certain meaningful behaviors. Working in the psychotherapeutic context, the therapist doesn't have the opportunity to observe directly the context in which sexual dysfunction occurs. Thus, the therapist is limited to what can be learned by eliciting descriptions of the "problem" from the client and by attending to the client's observable behavior and language patterns during the therapeutic sessions.

As regards the system formulation presented, the therapist seeks to know how certain external stimuli interact with internal processes to produce the undesirable experience, whether it be with an individual or a couple. So, besides detecting the client's lead and representational system and obtaining a full verbal description, the therapist also gathers the sequence of behaviors involved in the present state. By using his ears, eyes, and sometimes sense of touch, the therapist learns what client "expressions" are linked to the events that make up the present state. Those "expressions" include voice tone, body posture, accessing cues, muscle patterns of face and body, and particularly descriptive words.

In order to avoid mind reading your clients, it's important to describe these "expressions" in sensory experience terms rather than to interpret them. To describe an "expression" as "his hands gripped the arms of the chair, knuckes white, facial muscles tightened, breathing stopped, pupils dilated" is describing sensory experience: saying he was "afraid" is an interpretation of what these aspects of behavior mean to someone else. Although this may seem a tedious distinction, it is crucial to be able to detect subtlties in behavior that are not available when we simply attach labels to categories of behavior. It's not a description of sensory experience to say her voice was "enthusiastic." Rather, her voice became "higher in tone, faster in tempo, displayed more differentiation in intonation patterns." These are distinctions available to our senses. We then label them with a word like "enthusiasm."

I do not suggest that you limit yourself to talking only in such ways, but instead that you can and do utilize all the sensory distinctions available to you, especially in the therapeutic context. Frequently, a change in voice tone or a jiggling left foot can be a very meaningful communication.

By attending to the verbal as well as nonverbal communication presented by the client, the therapist learns about the sequence of external behaviors and internal processes that make up the client's present state. That is, what sequence of internally-and externally-generated experiences make the problem possible. Once the therapist has gathered information and knows what the present state is, it is useful to induce it in order to verify that it is, indeed, what and how it seems.

So, continuing with the previous example of Mary, there is the external stimulus (ES) of the sight or feel of an erect penis, which triggers the internal processes (IP) of picturing the uncle, which is represented consciously (RC) as feelings of terror, eliciting her external behavior (EB) of tightening up. Graphically, this sequence can be depicted like this:

triggers

ES ———————→ IP

IP ———————→ RC

RC ———————→ EB

External Stimulus = sight or feel of erect penis

Internal Process = picture of uncle

Represented Consciously = terror

External Behavior = tightening up

Since the client could not be presented with an erect penis, I induced this sequence by having the client visualize the last time she saw an erect penis. Once she made the visualization, she exhibited the same "expressions" elicited earlier in describing what happened when she was approached sexually. She went through the same sequence of accessing cues, voice tone and tempo changes, changes in breathing, and shifts in color and muscle patterns of face and body (tense thighs drawn close, arms tight to body). These changes in "expressions" were subtle to the untrained observer and most were outside of the client's conscious awareness.

The observed sequence of stimulus-response behaviors verified my understanding of the client's present state. It is important to remember that words are attached to experience as are memories, and people truly experience much of what they are talking about.

Mary would reexperience to a degree her past sexual experiences as she described them verbally. This was obvious by the changes in breathing rate, facial color, muscle tenseness, change in voice tone etc. Think about the last time you told someone about an experience when you had been terribly angry. Or better yet think of such a time now. Some of those feelings come back as you do this and the acute observer can detect the changes in breathing, lip size, face color and tension that those feelings bring.

The trained observer can make sensory distinctions that allow subtle nonverbal behaviors to become extremely useful communications. This is done not by labeling them, but by attending to how they relate to the process as a whole. For example: When do they occur? What happens just before the lower lip quivers and just after? How does this behavior make sense within the context of the problem?

So the therapist gathers information about the present state by utilizing sensory experience and the Meta-model to discover answers to the following questions:

1. What external stimulus triggers the unwanted experience?
2. What internal process does that external stimulus trigger?
3. What is represented in the client's consciousness?
4. How do these three categories relate to one another, and in what sequence?
5. Each time the external stimulus is triggered in some way by the therapist, does the whole sequence fire off again?

When the therapist knows the answers to these questions, and has a yes to number five, he has what he needs to decide upon a course of change.

Often the sequence and relationship of these categories are quite fixed and rigid for people. That is, something they hear (external stimulus) triggers a picture (internal process) which induces a feeling congruent with the picture (represented consciously) and their external behavior becomes congruent with their conscious representation. Frequently, a similar sequence is repeated for almost every experience. For example, they hear a harsh voice, picture their father yelling at them, feel frightened, act frightened. Or, they hear the description of a peaceful scene, picture themselves in that scene, feel peaceful and serene, and become outwardly calm and relaxed. There can be many variations of such sequences.

While this phenomenon can produce useful and satisfying experiences for the person in some instances, it may not in others. Therefore, the therapist can choose to enhance a client's experience by assisting him in gaining more successful ways of responding. Changing the sequence naturally serves to alter the system. A more limited goal would be to keep the same sequence while changing the type of response. Although the latter will give the client the desired state, the former begins the client on the road to developing generative personality by giving them more than one strategy for producing experience.

When making the distinctions presented herein you will almost always know more about the client's ongoing experience than the client himself knows consciously. Indeed in the course of everyday communication I am aware of people's language, accessing cues and other nonverbal behavior the way they are aware of the color of my hair. This added information greatly assists me in communicating effectively with everyone I meet, whether its the butcher, the insurance salesman or next door neighbor. If I told them what I see and hear that they are unaware of it would get in the way of our communication. Likewise, it is not necessary for the client to be consciously aware of the same aspects of behavior that the therapist must be aware of. Telling people's conscious mind about aspects of their behavior they were previously unaware of is called meta commenting (in therapy circles). Although a choice, it is not always the best one and can elicit a defensive response. The client can most often be unaware of aspects of his present behavior and still change in desired ways. The therapist's task, is to induce that change.

Notes

1. Representational Systems: "Each of us, as a human being, has available a number of different ways of representing our experience of the world. Following are some examples of the representational systems each of us can use to represent our experiences.

   "We have five recognized senses for making contact with the world—we *see*, we *hear*, we *feel*, we *taste* and we *smell*. In addition to these sensory systems, we have a language system which we use to represent our experience. We may store our experience directly in the representational system most closely associated with that sensory channel. We may choose to close our eyes and create a visual image of a red square shifting to green and then to blue, or a spiral wheel of silver and black slowly revolving counter-clockwise, or the image of some person we know well. Or, we may choose to close our eyes (or not) and to create a kinesthetic representation (a body sensation, a feeling), placing our hands against a wall and pushing as hard as we can, feeling the tightening of the muscles in our arms and shoulders, becoming aware of the texture of the floor beneath our feet, or, we may choose to become aware of the prickling sensation of the heat of the flames of a fire burning, or of sensing the pressure of several light blankets covering our sighing bodies as we sink softly into our beds. Or we may choose to close our eyes (or not) and create an auditory (sound) representation—the patter of tinkling raindrops, the crack of distant thunder and its following roll through the once-silent hills, the squeal of singing tires on a quiet country road, or the blast of a taxi horn through the deafening roars of a noisy city. Or we may close our eyes and create a gustatory (taste) representation of the sour flavor of a lemon, or the sweetness of honey, or the saltiness of a stale potato chip. Or we may choose to close our eyes (or not) and create an olfactory (smell) representation of a fragrant rose, or rancid, milk, or the pungent aroma of cheap perfume.

   "Some of you may have noticed that, while reading through the descriptions of the above paragraph, you actually experienced seeing a particular color or movement; feeling hardness, warmth, or roughness; hearing a specific sound; experiencing certain tastes or smells. You may have experienced all or only some of these sensations. Some of them were more detailed and immediate for you than others. For some of the descriptions you may have had no experience at all. These differences in your experiences are exactly what we are describing. Those of you who had a sharp clear *picture* of some experience have a rich, highly developed visual representational system. Those of you who were able to develop a strong *feeling* of weight, temperature or texture have a refined, highly developed kinesthetic representational system. An so on with the other possible ways associated with our five senses that we, as humans, have of representing our experiences."—from Bandler and Grinder, *The Structure of Magic II,* pp. 6–7

2. J. Grinder and R. Bandler, J. DeLozier, *Patterns of the Hypnotic Techniques of Milton H. Erickson M.D.* II (Cupertino, Calif: Meta Publications, 1977), pp 34–35

3. Masters and Johnson, *Human Sexual Inadequacy* pp 65–66

4. The Pairing Principle: "What we have noticed time and again is that the distribution of representational systems and Satir categories in family systems and in polarities is the same. Specifically, in Part II of this volume, we pointed out that the most frequent and effective incongruity-into-polarity sorting was a sorting which resulted in two polarities: one, a visual/Satir category 2 and the other, a kinesthetic/Satir category 1. Parallelly, in the context of couples and family systems work, the most frequent distribution of representational systems and Satir categories is one in which one of the parenting family members is a visual/Satir category 2 and the other, a kinesthetic/Satir category 1." —from Richard Bandler and John Grinder, *The Structure of Magic II* (Palo Alto, CA: Science and Behavior Books, 1976), p. 133.

5. R. Bandler and J. Grinder, *The Structure of Magic I* (Palo Alto, Ca: Science and Behavior Books, 1975), p. 95

6. R. Bandler and J. Grinder and J. DeLozier, *Patterns of Hypnotic Techniques of Milton H. Erickson II* (Cupertino, Ca: Meta Publications., 1977)

7. F. Farreley and J. Brandsma, *Provacative Therapy* (Cupertino Ca: Meta Publications., 1978)

8. R. Bandler and J. Grinder, *The Structure of Magic I* (Palo Alto, Ca: Science and Behavior Books, 1975), pp 13–14

9. W.H. Masters and V.E. Johnson, *Human Sexual Inadequacy* (Boston: Little, Brown and Co., 1970) p 142; pp 256–257

Part III

Techniques to Evolve
The Client from
Present State to
Desired State

Once the therapist understands the client's present state and knows what set of experiences would constitute the desired state, the task is to evolve the client from the present state to the desired state. It's important that the therapist has available a number of effective choices to accomplish this. Then a method can be chosen as to its appropriateness both for the client and for the specific problem content.

Overlapping

A fundamental method of evolving the client is to assist the client in generating rich full vivid internal experiences which involve all sensory modalities. Besides producing a profoundly altered state experience this develops the client's abilities to use his own internal processes as the resources they are, to generate needed experiences. Overlapping is a technique used to accomplish this. Overlapping begins with a verbalization congruent with the client's primary representational system and then adding the other sensory modalities. This is done by verbally using the natural points of intersection that exist between the senses.

If you are a highly visual person, for example, this process begins by your making an image of, say, a tree or grove of trees. Once you can see the trees clearly out before you, noticing the varying colors and shapes of leaves and branches, then—and only then— you can begin to observe the beginnings of movement, the gentle rustle and swaying of the leaves and branches. As you watch the leaves and branches swaying, you can begin to hear the sounds of the breeze as it blows gently through the trees, rustling the leaves. And, as you listen to the sound of the breeze whispering past, you can begin to feel its coolness as it brushes past your face. With the coolness of the breeze across your face, you can smell the freshness of the breeze as it wafts the fragrance of the trees to you.

So, in this example, beginning with the visual experience—the image of a tree—and then overlapping sensory experience at natural points of intersection, the person is able to expand the original representation to include all the sensory modalities of a vibrant, internally-generated experience. If you can see the wind moving the leaves and branches, then it's a short step to hearing the sound of the wind. Hearing the wind, surely it's also possible to feel it blowing across your face. And, if you can feel the breeze, it is only one more step to smelling the freshness of the breeze and the fragrance of the trees which you can see so very clearly.

In this way, our senses work together to create whole experiences. Starting from any of the sensory modalities and progressing through the natural points of intersection, a full, rich experience can be quite easily constructed. Our senses work this way naturally. It would be odd, indeed, to see a drop of water on your arm and not simultaneously feel its wetness and perhaps hear the sound of falling rain and smell the dampness in the air. Helpful to this process is the use of evocative words that are appropriate to the sense being described. The words listed below are those used in the preceeding example.

Visual	Auditory	Kinesthetic	Olfactory
see	hear	feel	smell
clearly	sound	coolness	freshness
image	rustling	brushes	fragrance
colors	listen	catch	
shapes	whispers		
watch			

Although overlapping representational systems is a technique that is effective in and of itself, it is often an integrated aspect of communication patterns designed to enrich a person's experience. It is especially useful with clients who are unable to focus their consciousness on the kinesthetic portion of experience in the sexual context. By beginning with whatever they do have in consciousness and adding the other modalities body feelings come into awareness and can then be emphasized.

In order for the natural sequence of internal and external processes that make up the successful sexual experience to take place, the kinesthetic portion of experience—i.e., body feelings—must be in consciousness. Most people, regardless of their most highly valued representational system, do become highly kinesthetic during sexual experiences.

Also overlap can be a valuable way of assisting those people whose internal processes interfere with their ability to fully sense the intense pleasure of the sexual experience. Overlap brings portions of experience that were outside of conscious awareness into consciousness and also serves to align the internal and external processes so that the experience becomes congruent.

In teaching the very highly visual person to use what he/she sees to lead them to their feelings, I have used overlap in these ways:

"Look at him. Do you see him clearly? Good, now as he leans closer and you see that very special look in his eyes, you can begin to wonder, really wonder. And as he comes even closer until you see his shoulder as his face is next to yours and you begin to hear his whisper. As he whispers, you can feel his breath as it brushes your ear, perhaps tickling it slightly. His words and his nearness change the rhythm and rate of your breathing."

"As you see her hand reaching over to you and then lightly touching, you can feel the temperature of her skin as it lies next to yours."

"While you listen to the tone of your voice, you become aware of the feelings behind it."

"As you see her look at you in that very special way, you can tell yourself how much she wants you and then feel how good it feels to be desired."

"As you hear the changing rhythm of your breathing, your excitement grows."

"As you watch yourself reach out and caress her, and notice when your skin meets hers, you become aware of the texture of her skin and as you move your hand and feel the

changes from one place to another, you can watch the expression on her face."

These are examples of giving the client instructions that use
the principle of overlap. For those clients who have not had a
successful sexual experience or who are terribly shy or inhibited,
I have found it useful to lead them through guided fantasies of
sexual experiences, using overlap and remaining maximally
vague, so that they are free to internally generate an experience
most satisfying to them. The art of remaining vague and yet specific enough to generate a rich guided fantasy is learned through
language patterns, particularly those found in *Patterns of the Hypnotic Techniques of Milton H. Erickson, M.D., Volume 1,* by Bandler
and Grinder. By remaining vague while directing verbalizations
toward positive experience the therapist can assist the client in
accessing the fantasy from internal resources rather than from
the therapist's own internal experiences. For instance, I might
say, "And there can be a certain sense of satisfaction in knowing
what you know." Now, "Certain sense of satisfaction" doesn't
specify what kind of experience that might be, and "knowing
what you know" does not specify the experience of knowing, also
leaving unknown "what" is known.

This method is especially effective with clients who typically say
"I just can't *see* myself doing that" when they are asked what stops
them from having the kind of sexual experiences they prefer. Such
a statement tells the therapist that their behavior would likely
change if they *could* "see themselves doing that." Since seeing
yourself doing something is necessarily an internally-generated
experience, it is quite appropriate to use guided fantasy, making
sure to employ the principles of overlap to insure a rich and full
experience.

Clients can be taught how to use their own internal processes to
enhance their sexual experience. Once the therapist learns how a
client generates body feelings (that is, whether they do so directly
or from words or pictures or sounds), he or she can then utilize
that information. For example, I mentioned earlier a female sex
therapist who complained of experiencing orgasm only with the
use of a vibrator. Upon investigation, I learned that when she was
making love her internal voices began to fret at her, saying "He's

getting tired, you'll never make it," and similar suggestions. When this occurred, she became worried and anxious which diverted her consciousness away from the current sexual experience.

Represented visually, her experience was:

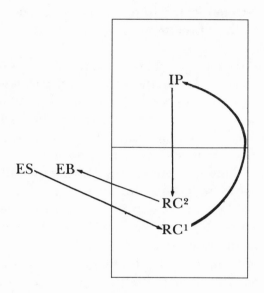

External Stimuli—Lovemaking—ES
Represented Consciously—Excitement—RC^1
Anxiety—RC^2
Internal Lead System—Voices—IP
External Behavior—Indicative of loss of Sexual Excitement—EB

It was important to her lover that she have an orgasm with him, and she also wanted this very much. But, because of the anxiety produced by the voices, they would repeatedly begin their love-making from the original excitement phase, over and over again, until the voices' description of his being tired and even bored finally were indeed true.

Although there were many choices for intervention in this situation, I chose to teach her how to use her internal voices to describe her current external experience: to describe where he was touching her, the warmth of his hands, the tenderness or strength of his touch, the sound and rhythm of his and her breathing, the beating of her heart. As she learned this, I also taught her how to use these internal descriptions to bring her closer to the experience she desired. That is, to verbally make a present experience lead to a desired one: "As I feel him moving with me, I can feel myself becoming even more aroused; breathing more and more rapidly, coming closer and closer to orgasm." (These verbalizations imply that "Since" she feels him moving with her she is becoming more aroused and "Since" she is breathing more rapidly she is coming closer to orgasm.)

Because this woman's emotional states were derived primarily from her internal dialogue, this method allowed her to feel desirous, aroused, excited, even orgasmic. It brought into alignment external sensory experiences and internal processes in such a way as to produce her desired outcome. Later, I was pleased to learn that, as she continued to use this process, the internal voices began to drop outside of her conscious awareness, leaving the fullness of the kinesthetic pleasures to occupy her attention. She also reported that she was able to induce other desired experiences— such as alertness, confidence, and a sense of calm—by employing her internal voices in the same manner.

I have also found overlap to be useful in assisting clients in the process of identifying with their partner's experience. Both men and women have frequently asked me what I thought their partners would like of them sexually. It's almost always been true that once they have had the internally-generated experience of "being their partner" and imagining what they would like to experience *from* themselves sexually, they have come up with appropriate and creative behaviors.

To use overlap to create this experience, the client imagines stepping into his or her sexual partner's body and then, beginning with their most typical representational system, uses the overlap principle to develop the full experience. So, they see themselves from their partner's perspective approaching, reaching out, hearing the sound of their own words, the tone of their voice, the touch of their own hands or body. Such an experience serves to give the client a source of incredible feedback as they fully imagine themselves from their partner's perspective. During the course of this experience, clients typically alter and adjust their own imagined behavior, making it more appealing from this new perspective. Of course, the client must use the direct sensory feedback offered by the partner in the actual sexual context to know whether his or her behaviors are indeed eliciting the desired response. Follow up reports from clients have indicated that their partners are most often delighted with their new behaviors.

This technique proved to be exceptionally effective with a woman client who came specifically for sex counseling. She complained that she always had to take the initiative with her husband sexually while he remained passive. Furthermore, he refused to join her for counseling and seemed content with how things were. During my initial session with this woman I used overlap to induce for her the experience of being her husband. As him she very much enjoyed the sense of being so desired and reveled in her own advances. The following week I received a call from her cancelling our appointment. When asked the reason, she said everything was "fine". She elaborated further that she had so enjoyed identifying with her husband that she shared the experience with him. She then asked him to imagine being her, which he did, and then to pretend *behaviorally* to be her. At first it all seemed silly and funny for him to act like her but she had responded so favorably that he had played the same "game" again later in the week. They were now taking turns being each other. This woman had surpassed even my expectations of results by creatively using her therapy experience to elicit the response she most desired from her husband. Since that time I have instructed clients who come without their partners in this and similar methods of eliciting desired behaviors on their own. When doing this I always use overlap to induce the client into a state of partner identification first, allowing this experience to serve as a foundation for their own subsequent actions.

Similarly, for some people, touching their mates while simultaneously imagining how this touch feels on their partner's skin is highly stimulating. This technique is especially appropriate with couples when one member has an aversion to oral sex. By imagining how their oral manipulation of their partner's genitals feels to them, it can suddenly become very exciting. In questioning clients who very much enjoyed performing cunnilingus or fellation, I found that this was in fact the strategy often used by them. In summary, these techniques of overlap and switching referential index can be used very effectively, either singly or in combination, and they form an important part of the therapist's ability to evolve the client system to achieve the desired state.

Anchoring

A basic premise of my work is that people have all the resources they need to make the changes they want and need to make. My job is to assist them in accessing and organizing their resources to make those desired changes an accomplished fact. Regardless of whether or not this basic premise is true in actuality, certainly when I structure my behavior as if it is true the results provide ample testimony to its validity.

The resources I am speaking of here lie in each of our personal histories. Each and every experience we have ever had can serve as an asset. Most everyone has had an experience of being confident or daring or assertive or relaxed, at some time. Each of those experiences is a possible resource. The therapist's task is to make those resources available in the contexts in which they are needed. Bandler, Grinder, DeLozier and I have developed a method called "anchoring" which does just that.

In the same way that certain external stimuli are associated with past experiences and can recall them, so can we deliberately associate a stimulus to a specific experience. Once this association has taken place, we can then trigger the experience at will. It works in the same way that language does.

If I ask you to remember a time when you felt very confident, a time when you felt truly satisfied with yourself, my words send you on a search through your past experiences. As you access various memories congruent with being confident and satisfied with yourself, various aspects of those experiences come into the present experience. Similarly, you know how you can become angry again by remembering a past argument or frightened again by remembering a terrifying movie or incident. Thus by bringing up a memory (an internally generated experience) we reexperience many of the same feelings which occurred when that memory was formed.

Anchoring utilizes this natural process by making a deliberate association between a stimulus and a specific experience. Examples of this that we are already familiar with are our responses to hearing the national anthem or seeing our flag, or perhaps our response to being given the "finger". The Russians may have understood this principle when after the revolution they kept all the melodies of their national songs and merely changed the lyrics. That is, the melodies were already associated to patriotic responses so merely changing the lyrics made the new associations nearly automatic. As an adult, have you visited a grammar school and been flooded with memories and feelings that were a part of your childhood? Can you remember the first time you were passionately kissed, really recalling the fullness of that experience and all the feelings associated with that kiss?

These are all examples of some aspect of your present experience recalling or triggering you to a past experience, such that your feelings become congruent with that previous experience. We have learned that by deliberately inserting some discreet stimulus such as a sound, a touch, a specific visual input or even a smell or a taste while a person is fully in touch with an experience, the stimulus then becomes associated with the recalled experience. So much so, if the timing is good, that reinducing the same exact stimulus brings back the feelings of the recalled experience. This procedure is called "anchoring". The specific inserted stimulus is referred to as the "anchor". The anchor then can be used to trigger the associated experience again and again. For instance if you and a partner were feeling especially romantic while a particular piece of music was playing, when next you heard that same music you would again be flooded with those romantic thoughts and feelings. "Your song would be playing." The concept of anchoring is that you could deliberately anchor such feelings in any chosen way and have them available whenever they were wanted or needed.

Vital to being able to insert a specific stimulus at the appropriate time (anchoring) is being able to identify when a person has accessed an important experience. In a previous section, the detection of external stimuli with relevant experiences was discussed. That discussion accentuated the importance of recognizing specific "expressions". Since you cannot know exactly what internal state a person is experiencing by their expression, you must depend upon your eyes and ears to detect the external expressions of an internal experience and be able to tell one from another. With anchoring, the specific areas that are useful to focus upon— because they change radically enough to be easily detectable—are voice tone, skin color, lip size, facial muscle tone, breathing rate and breathing from upper or lower chest. There are other changes as well, like skin temperature, but noticing these will be sufficient. By eliciting various intense responses that correspond to different internal states, you can recognize and differentiate a person's various experssions.

You can elicit various intense responses simply by asking them to access a series of various past emotions such as when they were last angry or frightened or passionate and then watch and listen for changes in the above areas and you will be able to detect the important differences. A person's lips may become thinner, facial color paler, breathing more shallow, when remembering a frightening experience, whereas lips typically are fuller, color flushed and breathing deeper with a softening of facial muscle tone when accessing passionate memory feelings. Your eyes and ears will become increasingly accustomed to detecting such minimal distinctions the more you do this. Should you detect no changes or very little change in your subject's responses check two things. One: is your own voice tone, facial expression, words, congruent with the response you are asking for? The more expressive you are the more expressiveness you are apt to elicit and your own behaviors need to be congruent with the response you are asking for. If you are asking for a passionate memory ask for it with an appropriate voice tone and facial expression. Perhaps a throatier, lower, sultry voice with a wink. Your success with anchoring is very dependent upon your own flexibility of behavior in that you will often be using your own expressiveness to elicit desired responses.

The second thing to check is whether your subject is remembering the asked for past experiences by being in the picture or by seeing themselves in the picture. Remember that seeing yourself in the picture is a constructed image and so can often be detected by noticing your subject's accessing cues. If you are not sure even by their accessing cues whether they are seeing themselves in the picture or not then ask them directly. This is crucial because if they are seeing themselves in the picture they will not be re-experiencing the past feelings. They will instead be experiencing feelings *about* the past experience. To exemplify, I would like you to picture yourself on a rollercoaster and see yourself in the first seat going up that first big hill so you are watching yourself on the rollercoaster. Then enter your own body in the picture so you can feel yourself sitting in that seat looking up, feeling the rollercoaster pulling you higher and higher, to the peak of that big hill. Just to the top, where you can see *all* the way down and feel your stomach rise as your body drops, listening to your own scream as you race towards the bottom. Obviously there is a big difference between the two images. The difference is crucial. If your subject is watching himself in that past experience you will not be anchoring the powerful feelings which would be occurring if your subject was inside his picture. If you discover that indeed your subject is watching himself merely ask him to step inside the picture and feel what he felt then, hearing the sounds which occurred then and seeing just what he saw in that past experience.

Once able to detect various expressions, you can anchor them. That is, while observing a full expression (an external representation of an internal experience) that having access to would be useful for therapeutic purposes, you can supply a stimulus to which the expression becomes associated. (This might be a touch on the back of the hand or a snap of the fingers.) With proper timing, firing off that stimulus will bring back the same expression, which means it brings back the associated internal state as well.

Many therapists already utilize this process by using a special voice tone and tempo when doing guided fantasy or hypnosis. This voice tone becomes an anchor for the altered states that are experienced when it is used. In Gestalt chair work, too, each of the two chairs becomes an anchor for a different emotional state and a client changes radically as he moves from one chair to the other.

In order to anchor a response successfully you should follow the following rules. (1) Have your subject access the desired experience or induce it as powerfully and fully as possible. (2) Insert your stimulus at the moment of fullest expression or most intense response. Timing is crucial! (3) Be sure your stimulus can be recapitulated *exactly*. Repeating the stimulus will only bring back the internal state fully if it is repeated exactly. Although I may describe anchoring as touching a client's knee or shoulder or the back of a hand, I want you to know that in actuality it is a far more specific touch. I repeat those touches exactly, even as to pressure. You can and should test these rules in your own experience both to verify them and to discover what *if any* leeway exists.

Using anchoring as described here gives the therapist access to a client's various experiential states. A common complaint concerning working with mentally disturbed people is that they change who, what, and how they are with great rapidity. As soon as a therapist is headed in a useful direction with such a client, his experience is that the client goes somewhere else. Anchoring can serve to steady the client's emotional state, allowing the therapist the opportunity to arrive at a desired goal.

Certainly, desirable sexual experiences can be anchored. Often couples already have useful anchors available to them. One man always knew he was in for a fantastic evening if his wife put on a specific nightgown. Seeing her in that nightgown aroused him immediately. Thus, the nightgown served as an anchor that triggered an arousal state in him. Another couple had set up cues to one another concerning their sexual desires that were based upon which side of the bed they got into. I have discovered that frequently women use a specific nonverbal behavior, a directed touch, which signals their mate that they are ready or eager for penile entry.

In cases of sexual dysfunction, too, there are anchors that trigger the unwanted experience. Often the anchor is outside of the person's conscious awareness, and they are aware only of the resulting unwanted experience.

A young woman, Melissa, came for therapy because of sexual dysfunction. She became absolutely petrified when men approached her sexually. When merely asked to describe her experience as a man approached her, she became terrified. So, I anchored this. Then, while using that anchor to trigger the same set of feelings I asked her to go back through her past and to describe other times when she had those same feelings. This technique of anchoring allowed me to take her back thru her personal history to a long forgotten childhood incident, a time when it seemed her mother had induced a male friend of the family to demonstrate seductive behavior toward Melissa. As he did so, her mother had forcefully impressed upon her the warning that a man who behaved in such a way intended to hurt her very badly, that this behavior meant that the man was dangerous and she was to run as fast and as far away as she could. Once this material was available to Melissa's conscious mind, it was quite easy for her to leave her mother's well-intentioned message behind. Melissa now believed that she no longer needed the protection such a message was intended to provide and that she could in fact protect herself from dangerous men in other ways. Using anchoring, we then accessed experiences from Melissa's past that provided more appropriate resources for realizing her present desires.

Anchoring With Couples

Anchoring can also be used to make desired responses more available to members of couples. When a couple comes for therapy their whole history of mutually-shared experiences is available as a resource. The fact that they are a couple indicates they wanted each other at some time in the past, perhaps, that they loved each other, that they had dreams about a good future. At the very least, they have gotten through some hard times together.

Anchoring allows me to access and employ these past experiences to build a better relationship for them now. And, if they are seeking therapy, now is just when re-experiencing the feelings that brought them together can be very useful.

For instance, if each time she gives him her sexiest come-hither look he thinks she looks funny, even ridiculous, then her come-hither look is not eliciting the response she desires from him. This, in fact, was exactly the case with a couple who came for counseling. Her tendency was to find men who would respond to her come-hither look as she wanted them to. Yet she loved her husband and stated she would be content if only he would respond in a manner that validated her sexuality. One choice at that point could have been for me to teach her to stop giving him that come-hither look and to find some new behavior that would better provide what she wanted. But changing external behavior is often a more long term goal, one that takes time and strong motivation on the part of the individual to achieve.

Another alternative, easier to effect, was simply to ask him to remember a time when he really felt she was sexy. Perhaps during their courtship, I don't know, but surely there was a time when he just couldn't resist her attraction. I chose this method and used analog behavior—voice tone, body posture, etc.—to help him remember a time when he really desired her. When I observed changes in his breathing, skin color and lip size, and heard changes in his voice tone and tempo indicating that he was indeed remembering such a time—and when I was certain that he was remembering it well enough to be actually re-experiencing those feelings of desire—*at that moment,* I inserted a discreet and covert cue (anchor) into his experience. Since my timing was appropriate to his remembered feelings, each time I used that cue he would again have that same experience. In this case, the anchor was a touch on the shoulder, which since I touch people frequently as I talk to them, could be gracefully repeated without distracting from the ongoing experience.

After ascertaining that the anchor worked by testing it, each time she gave him her come-hither look—which I had her do repeatedly —I triggered the anchor. By doing this, I was working to associate his experience of desiring her (which I could bring back by touching his shoulder) with her come-hither look. (stimulus-stimulus-response) Thus, I obtained the response that she wanted from him and associated it with *her* behavior. Of course, another choice could have been for her to merely touch his shoulder when she wanted him to know how much she desired him, thus giving him an opportunity to respond. My preference, though, was to access the desired experience in him as a response to her naturally-occurring behavior.

Anchoring also proved useful in working with a woman who participated in a workshop in Tucson. Her problem was that although she loved her husband dearly she was not sexually attracted to him. Much older than she, he did not fit the "Adonis" image she found stimulating. This problem had caused trouble in their otherwise very happy relationship for quite some time.

Since this woman generated her body feelings primarily from internal images—that is, she used a visual lead to a kinesthetic representation—I merely asked her to imagine the perfect male image and then signal by nodding her head when she had it. As she visualized various male bodies, the color of her skin flushed, her lips swelled, her breathing became deeper. As she began to nod, I reached out and touched her lightly on the right shoulder, saying, "Excellent, I'm sure he's very beautiful." Thus, I had associated my very specific touch on her right shoulder with the experience she had while visualizing the "perfect male physique." She was not aware of this consciously. Shortly thereafter, as we continued our talk, I again repeated the touch on her right shoulder to determine if the anchoring was successfully done. It was. The same "expression" that had occurred came back again. I then asked her to visualize her husband standing naked before her and to nod when she could see him clearly. As she began to nod this time, I said, "Good, now continue to look at him and notice how your feelings change as you see him in a new way." As I said these words, I again repeated the touch on her shoulder, triggering the response she wished to have with her husband. Her breathing became deeper, skin tone flushed and lips swelled as they had done before. I repeated this process twice more while we were together. When her husband came to pick her up at the day's end, I utilized his presence by instructing him privately in just how to touch her on the shoulder when he wished her to know that he desired her. As he touched her, I watched closely to make sure the anchor had transferred to include his touching her as well as her internal image of him naked. Soon the touch on the shoulder would not be needed because the experience of being aroused by the visual experience of her husband would have generalized. In the meantime, his special touches would continue to be meaningful. In this way, I utilized the process of anchoring to locate the desired experience (one of being aroused) and then associated it with the context in which this woman wished to experience it.

Changing History With Anchoring

Another client, Chuck, believed he was a complete failure with women, especially in the sexual context. Judging by his behavior, it was not difficult to concur in his belief. He had been in therapy for two years and had been referred to me by his male therapist, a psychologist who thought I would be especially effective in helping Chuck with this problem area.

Chuck was completely certain about his likelihood of failure with women in almost any situation, but he was acutely so concerning sexual encounters. He stated that his certainty was based on past experience and that he could not imagine things ever being different or better in the future. As we talked, I learned that Chuck's behavior was generally predicated upon past events. He used eidetic (that is, past) images to guide his present behavior. What he did well in life, he did very well—over and over again. He used these eidetic images as a lead system and then represented them kinesthetically as feelings about what he was going to do. So, whenever he came into contact with a woman he accessed visual images from past unsuccessful experiences with women and felt sure he was going to "blow it again." And, of course, he did. Thus, in order to quickly change his ongoing behavior with respect to women, I needed to alter these past eidetic images. To do this, I employed a method which utilizes anchoring that we refer to as "change history." The partial transcript which follows illustrates the use of this very important technique:

Therapist: Chuck, can you tell me again how you feel when you approach a woman?

Chuck: (As he answered, I watched closely to see if the same expression reoccurred that he had before when talking of women. Part of this expression was an up and left accessing cue.) Well, sure. If anything I'd like to forget it. But I just feel really shitty, you know.

Th: (When the expression was fully there, I touched him on the right knee, saying . . .) Good, it's important that you remember that feeling just now.

C: Oh, yeah. Why?

Th: You'll understand very soon. Now, take that feeling (I touched him again on the right knee and held it there watching the expression come back) that "really shitty" feeling, and tell me what scene from your past comes to mind.

C: Well, it's a time from a couple of years ago when I was out with this woman. I, uh, made a pass at her. Wow! It was a real disaster!

Th: I believe you. Now, what I want you to do is take that same feeling and go back in time. Back through your past and find other scenes in which you had this feeling.

C: (Closes eyes) Okay.

Th: That's right. And just go on back and I'll stop you sometimes.

As Chuck searches through his past on the pathway provided by this particular feeling, he remembers other experiences of which this feeling was a constituent. So while other portions of the experience change—like who was there, how old he was, what was said by whom, etc.—the feeling portion of the experience remains constant. While he was doing this, I watched for subtle exaggerations of the expression; greater intensity of skin color or deepening of lines in the forehead and around the mouth, tightening of the lips and changes in breathing. These exaggerations indicated that he was remembering especially intense experiences when this unpleasant feeling occurred.

Holding the anchor constant keeps the feeling constant and

insures that the search through time is done on the pathway of a
specific feeling. When I saw an exaggeration, I said to Chuck:

Th: There! Stop there. Take a really good look at that scene.
     Does it make sense to you in relationship to your feelings? (With
     my other hand, I mark out this specific experience with a touch
     on his other knee so I'll be able to come back to it later.)
C: Yes, yes it does.
Th: And how old are you there?
C: Oh, I was sixteen then.
Th: Good, good. Now, continue back just as you were.
Ch: Okay.

Again, I wait for the exaggerations. The moments slip by until
there is a very gross exaggeration of his expression:

Th: Stop there. Take a really close look at that scene. Tell me,
     how old are you?
C: I'm about six (voice quality is higher, more childlike than
     before).
Th: And what's happening to you there, Chuck?
C: I'm in parochial school. God, I hated school and I'm in trouble
     with the nuns. I don't know what for, but I really remember that
     somehow this was the first time I ever realized that nuns were
     women. I don't know what I thought they were before, but this
     is the first time I knew they were women.
Th: (Again, I marked this with a different touch on the knee,
     making it possible to facilitate his going back to this experience;
     then I take my hands from his knees.) Now, Chuck, I want you
     to come back here. Open your eyes and see me. Hi. That was
     quite a trip you took. Are you all the way back here now? Can
     you feel the back of the chair?
C: Yeah, sure, I'm here.
Th: Good. What I'd like you to do now is to think about what
     resource you would have needed in those experiences so that
     they would have been good ones, so that they would have been
     experiences that you felt really satisfied about.
C: What do you mean by resources?
Th: Like being confident or assertive or relaxed. If you had just
     been able to be assertive, say, then you would have acted differ-

ently and those experiences would have happened in a way that satisfied you instead of giving you that shitty feeling.

C: Well, what I needed was for the women in those experiences to like me.

Th: I agree; but, what could you have done to get them to like you?

C: I don't know.

Th: Do you get along well with men?

C: Yeah, pretty good.

Th: What resource do you have in dealing with men that makes it so different?

C: I don't know. I guess I'm just relaxed. Yeah, just real relaxed. I don't worry about what's going to happen. I just feel like it doesn't really matter.

Th: Good, good. That's what I'm after. Chuck, go ahead now and remember a time when you were really relaxed in the way you just described, a time when maybe somebody else would have been nervous, but you were really calm and relaxed (as I said this, I calmly leaned forward so I could reach his arm to anchor this experience).

C: Sure, I got one.

Th: Good (touching on forearm). Tell me about it.

C: I asked my boss for a raise and I was just as calm as could be. It didn't really matter what he said; I had nothing to lose so I felt really relaxed.

Th: Great (taking hand from arm). A lot of people couldn't have done that. You know those feelings of being really relaxed (touch arm again and I can see the "relaxed expression" come back).

C: Yeah?

Th: Well, what I want you to do is to take *THESE* feelings of relaxation back to those other experiences. So, starting with the most recent one that you took a close look at, I want you to take THESE feelings with you and notice how different everything is. (These feelings are kept present by keeping my hand on his forearm, thus using the anchor to fire off relaxed feelings) Notice how you behave with THESE FEELINGS and how differently those women respond.

C: Okay.

Th: Good. When you've gone through that first experience and are completely satisfied with it, and only when you are completely satisfied with it, I want you to nod your head. Now, go ahead.

C: (Time passes, and Chuck nods.)

Th: Excellent, and now I want you to go back to that time when you were sixteen (I trigger the anchor on the knee, with my other hand, which marks out that experience), and do it over again as you did with the last experience. And, again, when you've gone through it completely and are completely satisfied with it, just nod.

C: (Again, time passes and Chuck nods.)

Th: Excellent. Now, I want you to do the same thing with the last experience (I trigger appropriate anchor), the one where you were six and were dealing with the nuns. Just do the same thing that you did before.

C: (Time passes, and Chuck begins to frown slightly.)

Th: Oh, oh. What's happening?

C: I'm not sure, but I just can't quite make this one okay. It's better than it was, but I still feel a little shitty.

Th: That's okay. It just means you need some other resource. (I release the anchors by removing my hands) "After all, sometimes a six-year-old boy needs all the help he can get when it comes to getting into trouble with the nuns. Come back and let's figure out what else you need to take back there with you." (Chuck opens his eyes and returns to the here and now.) "Now, what do you think the six-year-old you needed?"

C: "Well, they made me feel like I was really bad, really bad and dirty."

Th: "But you know better than that now, don't you?"

C: "After two years of therapy, I should hope so."

Th: "Good. Now, tell me about a time when you did something, maybe something nice for someone else that made you feel like a *really good* person."

C: "Hmmm, let's see" (goes up and left). "Well, I, uh, helped my next door neighbor fix his car. I don't even know him, but he was having lots of trouble and I could see him out the window, and I just went out and gave him a hand. It took the whole afternoon, but I feel like that was a real nice thing to do." (As he describes this incident, I again anchor him on the forearm with my other hand.)

Th: "Makes me wish you were my neighbor. Now, you know those feelings of feeling really good about yourself, really knowing you're a good human being (trigger anchor)?"

C: "Yeah."

Th: "And those feelings of being very relaxed? (I trigger the "relaxation" anchor so I now have both hands on his forearm, simultaneously firing off both resource anchors.)

C: Yeah.

Th: Well, take ALL THESE feelings back and revisit the nuns and just nod when that experience has happened in a way that really satisfies you.

C: (Chuck closes his eyes. A few moments pass, and he grins broadly and nods his head.)

Th: (I let go of his arm) Great. Really makes a difference when you can take your resources where you need them, doesn't it?

C: It sure does. Those experiences just seem kind of funny to me now.

Th: Do they? Good. Then go back and remember them again and find out for sure.

C: Okay (closes eyes, sits quietly for a few moments; then smiles). Yeah, they weren't any big deal.

Th: Excellent. Now, when is the next time you're going to make contact with a woman, other than me, of course?

C: (Laughs) Oh, you don't count. You're a therapist.

Th: Thanks a lot, but when will you make contact with a woman that will be somehow meaningful?

C: Well, I won't unless I make one happen.

Th: When is your first opportunity to do just that?

C: Well, I could approach Sally. She's a girl at work that's single and attractive.

Th: Great. What I want you to do is to imagine how you'll approach her, but to be sure to take that sense of relaxation and those good feelings about yourself along, okay? (I am now using no anchors in order to learn if the changes that have occurred concerning past perceptions will generalize into future imaginings.)

C: Okay (closes eyes, sits quietly, gives a half-smile and chuckles).

Th: How'd you do with Sally?

C: Well, pretty good. I didn't make like Paul Newman or anything, but I didn't feel scared about talking to her.

Th: Fantastic. That deserves a handshake. So, you really felt okay
about talking to her. That's just great. (We ritualistically shake
hands. Thus shaking hands can also be an anchor for this successful internally-generated experience and may be triggered in
the future by a handshake.)

From this point, it was easy to assist Chuck with future projec-
tions and role playing; to be relaxed and comfortable about relating to women. By taking resources and incorporating them into a
context where needed, it is possible to change a person's history.
In a sense, Chuck's history had stopped him from expressing new
behaviors. Until his history was subjectively changed, he could
only continue to live out a predetermined present and future with
regard to women. Our personal histories are sets of perceptions
about past experiences and, as such, can be altered. Chuck used
his memories of the past to anticipate and even program himself
for the future. To a large degree this is true for all of us. With
Chuck, changing the past with respect to women in a way that
resulted in good feelings and a sense of satisfaction also allowed
him to change his present and future behavior. Just as only one
trauma easily generalizes to many associated contexts, I have
found that only a few important experiences need be changed for
generalizations to occur for other associated past experiences as
well. Changing history produced an alternate set of eidetic images
for Chuck to recall when he thinks about relating to women. Usually only one added resource is needed to effectively change history, but in Chuck's case the nuns were so powerful a memory that
a second resource was needed.

The tremendous effectiveness of changing history was discovered by paying attention to how people can distort their internally
generated experience and then act on the distortion, forgetting
that they created it in the first place. For instance, jealousy is an
experience almost always generated as the result of a person making constructed images of a loved one with someone else and then
feeling bad in response to the picture they have themselves
created. This picture and feeling are then acted upon just as
though they had been experienced externally. In fact, it is sometimes impossible to convince the jealous person that his or her
imaginings did not actually take place. Once a constructed image
is made, it can be stored and recalled as an eidetic image. Because

of this, a person must remember in some system other than visual that he or she created it.

Changing history is a utilization of this same process. The fuller and richer in detail the internally-generated history change is, the greater the possibility of it being given equal validity with the "real" history. Because of our ability to store experiences and draw upon them as resources, the changed history becomes an accomplished experience and thus can serve as a foundation for the future. The steps for this process are:

1. Anchor the unwanted or unpleasant feeling.
2. Use this anchor to assist the client in going back through time finding other times when he or she felt "this" way.
3. When exaggerations of the expression are noticed, stop the client and have them see the full experience, noting their age when the experience took place. With each exaggerated experience, establish an anchor so you can get back to the specific experience if needed (these anchors can be auditory or kinesthetic).
4. Once the client has identified three or four such experiences, release that anchor and bring them back to the present.
5. Ask the client what resource he needed to have in those past situations for them to have been satisfying experiences. Be sure the resource is one which influences the client's behavior and subjective experience. Many people, like Chuck, think everything would be fine if only the other people were somehow different. The point, however, is for the client to have been different and thus to make new learnings by eliciting different responses from the other people involved in that past experience. Once the needed resource is identified, assist him in accessing an experience where he genuinely exhibited that resource fully. Anchor it.
6. Using the resource anchor, have him go to each of the already identified past experiences and change history using the added resource. You can use the anchors which designate each of the three or four experiences to assist them in going directly to them. When he is satisfied with the changed experience, have him nod and then proceed to the next one. (If your client is not satisfied with the new outcome produced in the old experience move back to step 5. Get another resource or a different re-

source more appropriate to the specific past experience then proceed on to step 6 again.

7. Have him remember the past experiences with no anchors to discover if indeed those memories have subjectively changed.

8. When past experiences have been changed, have him future-pace. That is, to imagine the next time a situation similar to the past ones is likely to occur, suggesting he take the needed resource along. Use no anchors. This is a way of testing whether the changes have generalized.

This process gives the therapist a way of knowing what result he is going for, a way of getting that result and a way of testing the attainment of that result. For this technique, kinesthetic anchors are best because they can be held constant whereas auditory anchors are difficult to sustain and visual anchors are ineffectual if the client's eyes are closed. Should you be working with a client who cannot "see" his pictures, then use the process of overlap to bring visualizations into consciousness before proceeding with the change-history technique.

Visual-Kinesthetic Disassociation

There are some cases in which the aforementioned anchoring techniques are not sufficient. Specifically, sometimes clients who seek therapy are suffering from the results of a *severely* traumatic experience in the past. So much so that when anything associated with the trauma occurs in their ongoing experience they become overwhelmed by feelings that are pertinent to the prior episode. In short, they have a phobic response.

This was the case, for instance, with the woman mentioned earlier who had a phobic response to the sight of an erect penis. The case histories presented by Masters and Johnson cite a gentleman who walked in on his wife completing intercourse with her lover and was thereafter impotent with her. Each time he began to make love to her he would visually flash back to that unfortunate incident and again feel as he did then.

All phobic responses have this same form: an external stimulus serves to trigger feelings associated with a past or sometimes a future projected traumatic experience. This is not only the case with phobic sexual dysfunction, but is also true for phobias concerning heights, darkness, closed-in places, and so on. Often the past incident is unavailable to the client's conscious awareness. In such cases, anchoring—that is, going back through time as in the change-history technique—and then overlapping from feelings to visual and auditory modalities can serve to make the past experience conscious.

Occasionally it is difficult to find a subjectively positive experience powerful enough to counteract the overwhelming terror or grief typical of phobic responses. When this occurs, simple anchoring techniques are not sufficient. It then becomes necessary to find a way to take as much of the intensity out of the trauma as possible.

A way of successfully doing this is to assist the client in disassociating from the *feelings* connected with the trauma. Specifically, the three-place visual-kinesthetic disassociation technique is applicable to such cases. This process utilizes fully unique aspects of internal visualization. When people see themselves going through an experience they have feelings *about* what they see. If they visualize the experience as though they are in it, they have the feelings contained in the experience itself.

While my colleagues and I were investigating the relevance of accessing cues to human behavior we discovered that some people remembered their past pleasant and unpleasant experiences in these different visual ways. Unpleasant past experiences were remembered in constructed images (that is they saw themselves in the picture and thus had feelings *about* the past experience) whereas pleasant past experiences were remembered as eidetic images (they were in the picture and directly re-experienced the feelings from the past.) This natural unconscious process of sorting allows the individual the luxury of re-experiencing past pleasantries and disassociating from past unpleasant feelings while still keeping those experiences available to the conscious mind. In this way the conscious mind can learn from past traumas without re-experiencing them. Such people whose unconscious processes make the aforementioned distinctions recover fairly easily from unfortunate or unpleasant experiences. Because they can think back to them from a disassociated point of view the pain is lessened and the perspective is clearer.

Phobic responses occur when people actually re-experience the feelings that were present during the trauma. The technique of three-place-visual-kinesthetic disassociation employs the process described above and enhances it with added disassociation and anchoring. It involves having a person watch himself from a third position; which allows him to watch himself watching himself going through the traumatic experience. In this way, the person can remain comfortable while still remembering the experience because the kinesthetic (feeling) portion is disassociated from the visual memory. Since it was found that with just the two place disassociation found naturally occurring in some people was not enough to keep the phobic client from collapsing into the reality of the trauma, the use of the third place is added as insurance against the occurrence of this undesirable possibility.

I have used this technique countless times and for just as many different kinds of traumas. That it is an extremely effective therapeutic technique is confirmed by the following examples: A woman who had witnessed the death of her young daughter and was still immobilized by grief two years later was able to put the experience behind her and go on. A man whose first sexual experience had been painfully traumatic found it to be something he could smile at rather than something that continually inhibited him. I used this technique with each member of a couple seeking counseling after an experience that had been traumatic for both of them. She had had a double masectomy and when she first exposed her naked body to him he could not hide his shock from her. Taking each of them through this process greatly assisted them in re-establishing the tender sexuality that existed before her surgery. The following is a brief description of the use of this technique with a particularly difficult and dramatic case.

I was called in by the police to work with a woman who had been the victim of an especially brutal rape experience. She was unable to give the authorities any information concerning her assailant because any reference to the incident triggered such a psychotic episode that sedation was then required. She also reacted violently to being touched or handled by male hospital personnel, making it difficult for the staff to care for her physical needs. She refused to allow her boyfriend to visit her and became extremely upset when he came anyway.

Jessica had been in the hospital a bit more than three days when I came to work with her. During our first two sessions, one in the morning and one in the evening, I concentrated on establishing trust and rapport with her, and immediately began organizing powerful anchors with her for safety and comfort. With hypnotic techniques, I was able to assist her in recalling times of safety and security from her childhood and I anchored those experiences. She would sometimes say she didn't know if she could hold on, so I established her holding on to my arm as an anchor for feeling safe and for staying in the present experience.

Since I already knew that I would use the three-place visual-kinesthetic disassociation with her, I needed to be a powerful anchor myself as well as to have access to her own strong feelings of comfort and security. Only with these would I be able to keep her from accessing the feelings associated with the experience of being raped, which belonged in the past and not in her present experience. After our third session, I believed the necessary trust and the appropriate anchors had been established. Under the circumstances, we were doing very well.

The fourth session proceeded as follows:

Therapist: Jessica, you trust me, don't you?

Jessica: Yes. Yes, I trust you.

Th: Good, because I'm going to talk to you and I know that since you trust me, you'll be sure to hear what I say. Jessica, you're here with me in this room. And just you and I are here. You're sitting comfortably in the bed and I'm beside you. Can you feel my arm? (Jessica reaches for my forearm.) Feels good to hold on to someone, doesn't it?

J: Yes.

Th: You remember how safe you can be as long as you hold my arm. (Jessica nods yes.) Jessica, something happened to a *part* of you a few days ago. (In this case I used the description of a "part" in order to further disassociate Jessica from the incident.)

J: (Jessica begins to tighten and show a fear response.)

Th: Just hold on, Jessica. You're here now. Here with me, very safe. Take a breath and look at me. (She complies and visibly relaxes.) What happened, happened to just a part of you, not all of you. Do you understand? Just a part of you. And you're here now. (Jessica nods and continues to hold on to my arm.)

That part of you needs your help, Jessica. It needs you to make some learnings so it can be okay again. You're here now and safe with me, and you can be very strong and even very solid. But, right now, that part of you isn't and it needs you. It will be hard

for all of you to feel as good as you can feel until that part gets
the help she needs. You know I'm right here, don't you, Jessica?
Will you begin with me to help that part of you?

J: (Jessica nods her head yes.)

Th: Excellent. Now, Jessica, the last time this part of you was just
fine was right *before* something bad happened to her. What I
would like you to do is to see that part of you—her—out in front
of you. But see her the way she was *before* anything bad happened. Just nod to me when you can see her out in front of you.

J: (Jessica's pupils dilate, facial muscle tone relaxes. She is still
holding on. She nods.) Okay, I can see her.

Th: That's very good, Jessica. How does she look? Does she look
okay to you there? (indicating by gesture the location of the
visualization.) Can you see how she is dressed?

J: Yes. She's wearing jeans and a blue T-shirt.

Th: Good. Now keep her there and you feel yourself holding my
arm.

J: Yeah.

Th: Now, Jessica, I want you to begin to float outside of your
body just in back of yourself. So that you can see yourself sitting
here next to me. See yourself holding my arm and watching the
part of Jessica that needs help out in front. So you float outside
until you can see Jessica next to me watching the younger Jessica
out in front. You'll be watching yourself watching yourself.
When you can see yourself here with me, nod your head.

J: (Jessica becomes completely still, her breathing is more shallow, and her hand rests lightly on my arm. She nods.)

Th: (I reach over with my other hand and place it atop her hand
in order to anchor this *third-place disassociation*.) That's very good.
Now, you can begin to help *that* part of you that's *there* in front.
The slightly *younger* Jessica over *there*. Slowly watch as the scene
begins to transpire. Let *that* part of you show *you* what happened
so *you* can know how to help *her*. Making sure that *you remain
comfortable* watching *Jessica today* watch the *younger* Jessica go
through *that* experience that happened *then*.

As Jessica proceeded to visualize herself in the past experience
from the third place, I watched closely for any sign of her becoming associated with the experience; that is, having the feelings of
being raped instead of the feelings of being safe and comfortable

with me in the present. During the next few minutes I repeated several times the directions:

Th: *You,* Jessica, feeling comfortable *here, now,* as you watch yourself watching the *younger* Jessica over *there,* going through *that* experience. And *you're* learning. Learning what that *younger* Jessica will need from *you.*

Whenever I observed changes in breathing or tightening muscles indicating she was collapsing into the reality of the rape scene, I used the anchor on her arm to help her stay in the third-place disassociation and repeated the directions, emphasizing those words which reinforced the disassociative process: *her, there,* the *younger Jessica* (anything before the present is younger even if it refers to only four days previously); *you, here, now, Jessica of today, safe,* and so on.

As she proceeded, Jessica's eyes welled with tears and soon they streamed down her face.

Th: That's fine, Jessica. Watch yourself here with me, crying for *her.* She deserves your tears and when *that* experience is over and *that younger* Jessica from *then* is quiet, nod your head.

Jessica's tears were a response to what had happened rather than a reexperiencing of the assault. Jessica continued to cry silently, her eyes open and pupils dilated, staring straight ahead at the scene before her. At last, she nodded.

Th: Very good, Jessica. And I know you've seen a lot and I know you've learned a lot. Now, I want you to float back into your body —here, next to me—feeling your hand on my arm reminding you of safe feelings of now. When you are back inside, just nod again.

J: (Jessica nods.)

Th: All right, Jessica. You've just watched the younger you go through a dreadful experience. She needs a lot from you. Soon you'll go to her, take her in your arms, and hold her, reassuring her that you're from her future and that it's going to be all right. There are other people who will help, and you can reassure her that she will feel safe again. Jessica, she needs to know that you love her and care about her; that she is going to be okay. And, especially, that you appreciate her. She went through a very horrible experience and you can appreciate her for doing the very best she could. Are you ready to do that, Jessica?

J: (She nods, and is now beginning to sob. She reaches in front of herself, arms outstretched, and brings them into herself, rocking and sobbing, rocking and sobbing.)

At this point, I merely sit quietly beside Jessica, my hand on her back; and I find that I, too, have tears streaming down my own face. I feel that this has been a very important experience for Jessica and that it signifies a large step towards her full emotional recovery. At last, her sobbing subsides, she puts her arms around me, and I hold her for awhile.

During the following sessions with Jessica, I used the same three-place disassociation to help recover important information for the police concerning the assailant. She improved very quickly and her boyfriend proved to be helpful and supportive throughout. Our final sessions were used as premarital counseling for them.

The steps for utilizing three-place visual-kinesthetic disassociation are:

1. Establish a powerful anchor for solid comfort.
2. Holding the anchor, have the client visualize himself out in front in the very first scene of the traumatic incident, making it a "still-shot." So he is sitting there, next to you, seeing his younger self before him.
3. When he can see himself clearly, have him float out of his body so that he can see himself sitting there next to you watching his younger self. As such, there are now three of him. The visual perspective remains from the third place. Their actual body in the second and the younger self going through the trauma in the first place. When this three place disassociation is accomplished anchor it.
4. Now have the person run the experience through, making sure he remains kinesthetically disassociated from the traumatic incident by the use of anchors and by the use of verbal patterns which seperate out the three places—*him, there, the younger you, that experience, what happened then,* to seperate the younger traumatized self from —*you, here, today, watching yourself* etc.
5. When the experience has been completely seen, have the third place float back into second place. (So the visual perspective is

being integrated with the actual body position of the client)
6. Have the present-day person go to the younger one (the one who went through the traumatic experience) and reassure him that he is from the future, giving the younger self needed comfort and appreciation.
7. When the present-day person can see that the visualized younger self understands, have him integrate by bringing that younger part back inside his own body.

The following diagram will serve to clarify the steps involved.

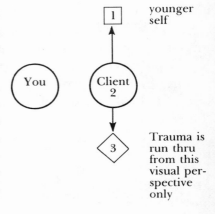

You anchor the client ② to feel secure in the here and now. Then the client visualizes his younger self ①, then floats out of his body to the visual perspective of ③. Anchor this disassociative state. From ③ the traumatic episode is run thru. After which ③ integrates back to ②. Then ② comforts and reassures ① and finally ② brings ① back into ② and only you and your client are there.

If at any time your client should collapse realities and begin re-experiencing the feelings contained within the past trauma, stop. Bring them back to the here and now completely, re-establish the first powerful positive anchor and begin again. In a few cases I have had to stop and start this process two or three times before the person was able to remain adequately disassociated such that the whole process could be completed.

This process is careful to disassociate when useful and then to fully integrate the disassociated parts of the person. This is a most effective method for dealing with those cases that involve a very powerful past experience that negatively influences a client's present experience. Clients describe this process as: "Bringing things into perspective," "I can remember it, but I'm not overwhelmed by it anymore," "I thought I just wanted to forget that awful thing ever happened, but now I think it's good; I learned a lot from it."

Association

The inverse of the process just described is useful for clients suffering from loss of body sensations; those cases, for example, involving a woman who feels nothing in her entire pelvic region or a man whose impotence stems from experiencing only numbness in his penis. With such as these, I have found it very effective to have the person visualize themselves very clearly and to have their visualized self be quite obviously enjoying the sexual experience. When they can really see themselves responding with full sensation (in the man's case, seeing himself with a full erection), I then have the person feel himself or herself floating over and into their own visualization. Thus, they associate the kinesthetic portion of the desired visual experience by "stepping into the picture."

The association process then is the inverse of the visual kinesthetic disassociation process. The client visualizes himself in a scene and adjusts the picture until it is just right for him. He then steps into himself in the picture in order to feel the feelings which are congruent with the projected experience.

This is also an exquisite technique for accomplishing self-image changes and for preparing a client to express new behaviors. It also serves as an education tool. In leading seminars I often ask participants to picture themselves interacting in their idea of a "perfect" relationship. When they have such a picture, to then step into themselves and notice how it feels. Does this indeed feel like a "perfect" relationship or should they change their image of what such a relationship is like? If it does feel like the "perfect" relationship then to memorize those feelings such that their behavior might lead them to actualize such a fantasy.

Besides Touching

Thus far in my presentation of anchoring I have primarily discussed the use of kinesthetic anchors. Because touching is a natural aspect of my own communication patterns this form of anchoring comes easy to me. I find other advantages to touching anchors in that they can be held and thus the effect sustained more readily than visual or auditory anchors. In terms of teaching the process in seminars my specific touching can be made obvious to the audience and facilitates the teaching process. Also when transferring the use of an anchor to the client/s, a touch can be repeated by another person with greater accuracy than a voice tone or visual facial expression. Thus increasing their ability to use that anchor.

However, there are special properties of visual and auditory anchors which make them preferable to some people and in some contexts. Richard uses changes in his voice tone and tempo as auditory anchors almost entirely. Because such shifts are subtle to all but the most trained ear these anchors remain far outside of conscious awareness. Such abilities to purposefully alter voice quality come easy to Richard whereas I have spent much time learning to bring such subtle aspects of my behavior under my own conscious control. I was impressed by the usefulness of such an ability years ago during a session with a couple. Richard and I were working with them together and I noticed that he was using the husband's tonality and intonation patterns in his own voice to anchor the wife each time either of us elicited a powerful positive response from her. Thus the husband's naturaly occurring tonality and intonation patterns would and did continue to elicit positive responses from his wife. In this way a general and pervasive mood change between them was accomplished.

Auditory anchors can run the gamut from these subtle voice changes to pencil tapping, chair squeaking, music, or even clock chiming. The importance is the timing and being able to repeat the same auditory stimulus at will.

Likewise, there are special properties which make the use of visual anchors most appropriate for certain people and certain contexts. Certainly in situations of potential violence a visual anchor is more appropriate than a kinesthetic one since getting close enough to touch could be dangerous. While working with a woman whose husband was prone to violent reactions I taught her how to take an impressive Karate stance. (Her husband was not participating in therapy.) I then gave her instructions that should a violent situation seem iminent and she could not get away or feel as if she could adequately defend herself to take that stance. Such a situation did arise and she did take the stance. Her description of her husband's reactions was that he stopped cold, looked confused and then burst out laughing. I did not know this would happen specifically but was going by the rule that new and different behaviors will elicit new and different responses. Because this stance elicited such a useful response from her husband I instructed her to use it whenever tensions began to mount. Thus it became a useful visual anchor which elicited humor from her previously angry husband.

So anchoring in any modality can be useful. The guidelines to use are; How appropriate is the anchor to the context? How easily can it be repeated? Can it be done as a naturalistic behavior and thus integrated into the ongoing interactions?

Reframing

The foundation which lies beneath the processes of reframing I am about to present is that every behavior, internal and external, every symptom and communication is useful and meaningful in some way. Contained within the structure of reframing is the belief that people have all the resources they need to make any desired change. This may or may not be true. What is important is that when I organize my behavior as though it were true positive change becomes easier to accomplish. Remember that we humans never experience the world directly but instead create maps or models of our world experience such that the only reality we shall ever know is a subjective reality. Utilizing the philosophy above is a terrific advantage since subjective realities can be altered and reorganized. We are given the opportunities to mold our realities in useful and beneficial ways.

So that this may be clear to you in a concrete way I would like to present a typical example of how I use this belief to produce change in my clients' subjective realities. During a seminar in New York a couple asked for help with a very specific and somewhat unusual problem. It seemed that the carpeting in their house was very plush and showed every footprint. Now this was, of course, not a problem in and of itself but the woman was compulsive about vacuuming the carpet so no footprints showed. Since everytime anyone walked on it there were footprints she did alot of vacuuming. This drove everyone crazy, and was a source of tremendous tension between her and her husband. Everytime she looked at the footprinted carpet she felt bad and did not feel good until she had vacuumed it. Having been presented with this description I asked myself how can footprints on the carpet be experienced as a positive occurrence by this woman so that she will not feel the need to constantly vacuum? This question made the task an easy one. I asked her to close her eyes and see her carpeted home. And to see that the carpet was perfect, not a single strand of it out of place. And as she was enjoying seeing the carpet so perfect I told her she could become aware that there was also complete silence in her house and as she listened to the silence she could realize she was *all* alone. Her loved ones were gone and she was *all* alone with her perfect carpet. It was only now, I told her, that she would finally realize that every footprint that appeared on that carpet was a sign that her loved ones were near, that she was with her family. So each time in the future, whenever she would see a footprint on the carpet she could feel the closeness of her family and the love she felt towards them. Like Mother's day presents saved year after year each footprint could be looked upon warmly. After all, I said to her, whose small or large foot had stepped there for her to see.

Thus I reframed "footprints on the carpet" to trigger warm loving feelings rather than compulsive cleanliness. As strange as this may sound it worked with her and really it makes more sense to feel good about footprints than it does to feel bad about them.

Besides this implicit form of reframing there are very specific and explicit techniques of reframing developed by my colleagues and me to accomplish positive change. These techniques can be integrated into a client's behavior such that he or she can accomplish personal change without need of a therapist. While other therapeutic and conflict resolution methods work with the content of the individual problems these explicit reframing techniques work to reorganize a person's internal processes into integrated resources such that any internal conflict can be resolved. This is accomplished by providing for the maximum employment of resources and flow of communication within that person. We refer to such a reorganized person as being generative; They are capable of generating new behavior and even a new reorganization of self should the need or the desire arise.

In comparison with other therapeutic models, which are implicitly methods of organizing human beings such that the complexity of behavior is reduced so the therapist can more successfully cope with it, reframing is a method of organizing the organization of human systems. Therapeutic models that are concerned with accomplishing a particular change or resolving a particular conflict ignore the possibility of constructing a generative system that can resolve future conflict and induce future change on its own. With reframing, a particular change is achieved or a particular conflict is resolved by a process that can be generalized to other contexts and integrated into the ongoing behavior of the human system, whether that system is an individual, a couple, or some other type of human systemic organization.

"Separating Intention from Behavior"

There are essentially two types of reframing. The first to be presented is separating the intention from the behavior. The process of separating intention from behavior is comprised of six explicit and sequential steps:

1. *Identify the behavior.* Identifying the specific unwanted behavior or symptom. The behavior may be any physiological symptom or any action that the client cannot stop himself from exhibiting. Or it might be a behavior that prevents or inhibits the client from acting in a desired way.

2. *Contact the part that generates the identified behavior.* Here begins the building of a bridge between conscious and unconscious processes. The client uses his own internal dialogue to ask, "Is the part of me that generates this behavior willing to communicate with me?" Then he is to pay exquisite attention to any response —any sound, picture, feeling, or words. The therapist also watches for any noticeable behavioral response of which the client may be unaware.

   If the response is other than words, it is important to make the communication as unambiguous as possible. This can be accomplished by establishing an intensifying of the response as a "yes" and a diminishing of it as "no." So, a brighter picture or a louder sound or a stronger feeling would indicate an affirmative response. If the behavior is a symptom, utilizing it as a means of communication is most effective; if the symptom is numbness, for example, having it spread to indicate "yes" and diminish to indicate "no."

3. *Separate intention from behavior.* Once communication has been established, the task is to discover the intention behind the behavior. Thus, the client asks, "What are you trying to do for me?"

Again, the answer may come in pictures, words, or feelings. If only feelings occur and it's impossible to make sense from them, use overlap to build a more complete representation.

Sometimes the answer will seem to be an undesirable intention, like "I'm trying to kill you" or "I'm keeping you from having sex." When this happens, take another step back by asking, "What are you trying to do for me by killing me?" This allows you to obtain a more useful answer, such as "I'm trying to save you from this miserable life that just keeps dragging on" or "If you have sex, you'll get hurt and that will be bad." Thus the extra step back reveals the intention to be one of protection. Always continue to step back until the "true" positive intention is discovered.

4. *Find three new ways to satisfy the intention.* This is most commonly done by accessing the person's creative part and having it generate three new, more satisfying ways to accomplish the intention. If the person doesn't have a creative part, build one. This can be done by having the client remember a time when he has been creative and then establishing an anchor that gives access to his creative part. If he claims he has never been creative, ask him if he knows of anyone he considers creative. After he says "yes", have him imagine that person visually and auditorily and then have that imagined person generate three better ways to satisfy the intention (of course, the answers are still generated from the client's own internal processes, but this technique can serve to bypass feelings of "I can't do it."). The least desirable choice, but still a choice, is for the therapist to suggest possible alternatives to the client.

5. *Have the originally-identified part accept the new choices and the responsibility for generating them when needed.* The client now asks the original part if it agrees that the three new choices are at least as effective as the original, unwanted behavior. If it says "yes" (using the pre-established mode of communication to insure continuity), ask if it is willing to accept responsibility for generating the new behaviors in appropriate contexts.

If it doesn't agree that the new choices are better than the original behavior, ask it to go and work with the creative part to come up with better ones. If it won't take responsibility for generating the new behaviors (this *very* rarely happens), access a part that will.

6. *Ecological check.* For the final step, instruct the client to ask inside if any part objects to the negotiations that have taken place. If there is an affirmative response, be sure to establish that it is a "yes" response by following the procedure described in step two. If there is an objection, cycle back through by identifying the objection, separating intention from objection, and so on through the steps. When there are no objections during the ecological check, the process is complete and success assured.

If, as sometimes happens, the identified part refuses to communicate in consciousness, the following steps, which bypass the client's conscious awareness, can be substituted.

Step 2. Even a "no" response is a communication and can be utilized. So, contact has been made.

Steps 3 and 4. Ask the part if "it" knows what it's doing for the person. If it answers "yes," have it go to the creative part on its own and get three new ways to do it better. Just have it signal in a specific way when it has accomplished this.

The rest of the steps require only a yes/no response and the conscious mind need not know the specific content of the new behaviors. Often, this experience provides the client with a foundation for greater respect and appreciation for his unconscious processes since changes occur without conscious intervention.

In rare cases, a part may respond negatively, saying it doesn't know what it does for the person. After you have asked it if it's sure of this, you can then directly ask it to *stop* generating the undesired behavior. In all my experience with reframing, such a response has only occurred once. The part said it had forgotten what the intention was; it complied with the instructions, though, by stopping the unwanted behavior (bedwetting).

"Contextual Reframing"

The second type of reframing is contextual reframing, which accepts *all* behaviors as useful in *some* context. In this process, the task is to identify the context in which the behavior is appropriate and to attach the behavior there. The steps are the same as previously outlined, except step three becomes establishing the useful context and step four is necessary only if the part generating the behavior doesn't know of any appropriate context. When this occurs, the creative part can be called upon to generate possible appropriate contexts. In step five, the part accepts responsibility for generating the behavior in *only* the accepted context/s.

"Application of Principles"

The following transcript demonstrates the use of a combination of these reframing techniques with a client, Tom, who suffers from impotency:

Therapist: Now, Tom, I know that the part of you that is keeping you from responding is trying to do something positive for you. So, what I want you to do is to go inside and ask what that part of you is trying to do, paying close attention to any words, pictures, sounds, or feelings that occur.

Tom: (Closes eyes momentarily, body pulls back as if avoiding being struck.)

Th: So what happened?

T: I asked the question, but nobody answered.

Th: Oh yes, they did; what happened?

T: Well, I saw my mother just like she was when . . . well . . . you know. (Tom was seduced by his mother while still in his teens and was unable to perform adequately; this inadequacy has continued to the present.)

Th: And . . .

T: And nothing . . . I had the same feeling I always do when I remember my mother that way.

Th: And you don't think that picture and the resultant feeling had anything to do with the question you just asked?

T: Well, when you put it that way . . . but my mother is dead and gone. What's that got to do with me now?

Th: She's dead and gone, but the picture isn't. Now, go inside and ask if that part of you will tell you what it is trying to do for you. If the answer is yes, have it show you the same picture again. If no, have it do something else.

T: (Goes inside, shows same involuntary pulling back.)

Th: Good, the answer is "yes."

T: How did you know?

Th: It was easy. Ask it to go ahead and tell you.

T: (Goes inside for a few moments and then opens his eyes but sits quietly for a few moments more.

Th: Well?

T: It says it's trying to protect me from my mother.

Th: Do you agree that you needed protection from your mother and perhaps things connected with your mother?

T: Yes, sure.

Th: Like what?

T: She was a dreadful bitch. Castrating. She would've destroyed me.

Th: Oh, so you agree that you needed protection from her.

T: Yeah, but . . . but how's not being able to get it up going to protect me from her. And she's dead now.

Th: I don't know. Can you *see* how it may have protected you from her then?

T: Hmmmm (eyes up-left, right, left). Yeah.

Th: Like it or no, there are parts of you that believe you still need protection from being destroyed or castrated or however you want to talk about it, right?

T: Yeah, but not like that.

Th: I want you to go to your creative part and ask it to suggest three *other* ways to protect you.

T: My creative part?

Th: Yes, I know you have one. Just go inside and give it a chance to do its thing. It may respond in pictures, words, feelings, or such, and *you* may not understand, but just pay exquisite attention to your experience.

T: (Goes inside for awhile; nods head once, twice, three times; smiles.) Okay. I got it.

Th: Oh yeah. What have you got?

T: Well, I asked inside like you said and at first nothing happened. Then I started seeing these short movies. I saw myself punch her out, really smack her up the side of her head. Then another picture of me walking out on her. Right out the front door. Then, best of all, I just laughed in her face. Ha, ha, ha, ha.

Th: Great. Those sound like much better choices. By the way, who was in your pictures?

T: Why, my wife—(pause)—of course. Wow, my wife.

Th: Hmmm, how 'bout that? Well, never mind that now. Let's go on. Now, I want you to ask the part of you that made you impotent in the first place if it agrees that these are more useful ways of protecting you. Pay attention to your experience. If the answer is yes, have it show you a picture of your mother again.

T: (Goes inside) It said yes. Can't we give it another way to say "yes"? That is so unpleasant.

T: Of course. Ask it to say "yes" another way. Perhaps a warm, tingling sensation along your midline.

T: (Goes inside, comes out smiling) Okay.

Th: Now, ask it if it is willing to generate those new behaviors for you whenever needed. Since it is the part that generated the original problem, it already knows when you need those behaviors. Right?

T: Right.

Th: Wrong.

T: Huh?

Th: Wrong. Unless you consider sexual encounters as the time to smack your mate, walk out on her, or laugh in her face. (Moving from seperating intention from behavioral reframing to contextual reframing.)

T: Oh, yeah. But it would have been good to do with my old lady —I mean, my mother.

T: Yes, but that was then, not now. How can you tell when it's time to protect yourself from those things your mother tried to do to you?

T: You mean did do to me . . . I don't know.

Th: Go inside and ask your creative part to show you situations when you need to use those behaviors.

T: (Goes inside for awhile, facial expression changes, color becomes redder, frowns, lips tighten, comes out.) Okay.

Th: Okay. So, how do you know when it's time to use those behaviors?

T: (Eyes down, right) When I feel pushed. When someone is trying to take advantage of me. You know, when they're trying to hurt me, make me do something I don't want to.

Th: When they're trying to make you do something you don't want to. Okay. So, go back and ask if that part—the first one— agrees that when you feel "that" way, *pushed,* that it's time to generate the smacking, walking out, or laughing behaviors?

T: Okay. (Goes inside.) I can't remember what to ask it.

Th: (Repeats directions given above.)

T: (Goes inside, smiles.) It says "yes." I think it understands this better than I do.

Th: Let's hope so (smiling). It's the one that really counts. So, ask it if it will generate the new, more useful behaviors at the appropriate times instead of the old one. You know the old one—"impotence."

T: Okay. (Goes inside.) It answered with the warm feeling. What if I just get that warm feeling and it doesn't really mean anything?

Th: Distrustful S.O.B. aren't you? Ask it a question you know it will answer "no" to, and find out what happens.

T: Okay. (Eyes up, left; then closed, taking on Tom's usual "go-inside" posture; comes out, laughs.) Well, it sure didn't give the warm, good feeling; that's for sure.

Th: Oh yeah, want to tell me what you asked it?

T: No (reddening). I think I'll keep it to myself.

Th: Well, do you believe it now? Ask if there is any part that has any objection to the negotiations that have taken place.

T: Okay. (Goes inside.) I got a queer feeling.

Th: Ask if the queer feeling means there's an objection.

T: (Goes inside.) I got the queer feeling again.

Th: Wait a minute. Ask if all your parts are satisfied with what took place.

T: (Goes inside, smiles.) I got the warm, good feeling.

Th: Ask if that means "yes" to give the same answer.

T: (Goes inside, smiles.) It or they did.

Th: Good, we have to be careful about keeping yeses and nos separate. Well, this means it's *time* for you to have a *coming out party* if you know what I mean (laughter).

But, I want you to wait for at least a week while your parts *get used to the changes.* And, no matter how much you *respond,* to wait until you can *wait no longer.* For, *you* are now going *to begin* to learn new, more delightful ways of responding to sexual stimuli. With no need for the old ways, they will be replaced. But we'll talk about that then.

With Tom, reframing served to allow a much despised behavior to make its usefulness known to him. Tom's impotence could be seen by him as being useful in protecting him from what his mother might do to him. Although he still needed protection at times from people other than his mother, he was able to find that more useful behaviors were available to him, which were presented by his own internal resources. Still, the timing for such behaviors was not yet appropriate; the new behaviors needed to be the result of appropriate stimuli. So, this transcript demonstrates an integration of the two processes of reframing: 1) separating intention from behavior; and 2) finding the appropriate context.

When reframing is done with a more-than-one-member human system (a couple, for instance), it follows the same steps already presented, but additionally uses the other member(s) of the system as creative resources. The following partial transcript of a couple-counseling session illustrates the use of reframing in this therapeutic context.

Therapist: Tony, what would you like changed with your wife and you to make you happy?

Tony: I'd like her to stop her bitching and nagging me all the time.

Th: And you, Nancy, what would you like changed?

Nancy: Him.

Th: Yes, but what—specifically—about him? Pick something to start with.

N: His constant moping and whining. I can't stand it.

Th: Okay, you want him to stop moping and whining and he wants you to stop bitching.

T: So we trade?

Th: I don't think that would work for very long. Tony, I want you to really think about this very carefully. What is it you would really like Nancy to do when you're moping around? Now, really think about it and tell me when you have an answer.

While he's doing that. I'd like you, Nancy, to do the same about your nagging.

N: Oh, that's easy. I want him to get off his ass and do something around the house.

Th: So, what you're really after with all that nagging is to get a helpful response out of Tony. Is that right? (intention separated from behavior)

N: Yes.

T: Well, what I really want is some support from Nancy for her to understand how tired I get and not to pressure me.

Th: So, when you're moping about, what you're really after is some support?

T: Yeah.

Th: How, specifically, would you like Nancy to support you?

T: You know, maybe put her arms around me, pamper me a little, make me feel appreciated.

Th: So, if she came and put her arms around you and pampered you, talked to you—nice things like that—you would feel supported by her. Right?

T: Yeah, I would.

Th: Well, what I know is that right now the way you let her know that you want her support is to mope around. And your moping around just makes her want to nag and bitch at you. Right, Nancy?

N: Right.

Th: Now, wanting to be supported is fine and getting that wanted support is important. But you've been doing just exactly the right thing to get nagging and bitching and just the wrong thing to get supported—at least by Nancy. So—congratulations—you now have the perfect way to get Nancy to bitch at you.

T: Oh, thanks a lot.

Th: Would you like some ways to actually get from Nancy what you *do* want?

T: Of course, but I'll be damned if I know how.

Th: I believe you. But there's someone in this room who could tell you exactly how to get the support you want.

T: So tell me already.

Th: Oh, I don't know but *she* does. Nancy, what is it that this man could do that would get him the needed support? Only you know. (Nancy is used in the same manner as a creative part)

N: Well, I never thought about. . . .

Th: Now's your chance: you can tell him how to act instead of that moping. He was just moping to get your attention, but the attention he got wasn't the kind he wanted. So, what could Tony do that would get you to put your arms around him, pamper him a little. You know, that sort of thing.

N: Well, if he was just nice to me.

Th: Let's be more specific. Can you remember ever feeling like
     you wanted to do just what it is he wants?

N: Well, sure, I must've sometime.

Th: That's right. And what did he do to get you to feel like doing
     that?

N: I'm not sure he ever did this, but if he would just come and
     put his arms around me and tell me he's dead tired or wiped out
     and that he needs me, I'd fall all over myself pampering him.

Th: Great. Listen to that, Tony. There's your answer. Can you do
     that? Put your arms around her and tell her you're dead tired
     and you need her?

T: Sure, I can do that; it just never occurred to me, that's all.

Th: Do you know when you need that support, Tony? I mean, do
     you have a way of telling when it's time to get yourself some
     support now, instead of time to mope? (establish context to
     generate new behavior)

T: Oh, yeah. I know that. I can really feel it when things are
     slipping out from under me. That's when I need support.

Th: That's beautiful. So, do you both think this new arrangement
     is better than the old one?

T: Yeah.

N: Yeah.

Th: Good. Now, about that nagging. . . . (The reframing process
     continued with Nancy utilizing Tony as the creative part.)

"Communicating with a Symptom"

As mentioned before, it is possible to use reframing to rid a
person of problematic symptoms by establishing communication
with the physiological symptom. In the following example, Carol
came to therapy seeking help to alleviate recurring headaches.
Probably everyone suffers from headaches now and then, but
Carol's headaches formed a significant pattern. They occurred
when she was in a situation that involved being alone with a man,
and disappeared when this situation changed. Except in this particular context, Carol was calm and adroit in social situations.

Knowing that such a systematic behavioral pattern constituted a
meaningful communication from her unconscious processes, I
chose to use reframing with Carol. I began by giving her these
instructions:

Th: Carol, can you remember the last time you were alone with a man?

C: Yes (her eyes drift down and right, her forehead and temples obviously contract as well as the muscles around her yes).

Th: And, as you remember, do you also re-experience some of the headache?

C: Yes. God, yes; I do.

Th: Good. Look at me and tell me when it's gone.

C: (She complies; in a few moments her muscles relax and her forehead again becomes smooth.)

Th: Carol, I want you to use your internal dialogue and go inside and ask, "Is the part of me that gives me the headaches willing to communicate with me in consciousness?" Then, I want you to pay attention to any feelings, pictures, sounds, or words that occur—any response whatsoever. Go ahead.

C: Okay (her eyes go down and left, and then again the same facial muscles contract).

Th: Good. I can see that it responded.

C: Well, I got a twinge of my headache if that's what you mean.

Th: Excellent. You couldn't ask for a better response. (It's preferable to use the symptom as the vehicle of communication. It provides assurance that communication has been established with the appropriate part or unconscious process.)

Now, we must make sure that we understand that part of you correctly. So, I want you to go inside and say, "If this feeling in my head means 'yes', you are willing to communicate with me in consciousness, then intensify the feeling; if no, then make it go away." Okay. Do you understand?

C: Yes, I do. (Carol closes her eyes and soon the same muscle contraction occurs. These muscle contractions now serve as a visual means for me to know what answers Carol is getting; she is experiencing the same phenomenon kinesthetically. Shortly, Carol opens her eyes.) It intensified the feeling.

Th: That's good. Now, we have a way of explicitly communicating with that part. Go inside and thank it for communicating with you.

C: (She complies.)

Th: Now, go inside and ask it if it would be willing to tell you what it is trying to do for you by giving you the headaches.

C: (Carol nods, and exhibits her going-inside behavior. Again, her facial muscles contract.) I got the pain again, so I guess it is willing to tell me. It's hard for me to believe it's doing something good for me.

Th: I believe you. But I know that it is. All your behaviors are meaningful in some way. Go inside and say "thank you" again and ask it to go ahead and tell you what it is trying to do for you. It may tell you in words or pictures—whatever.

C: Okay. (Goes inside for several moments.) Hmmmm.

Th: Did you understand its answer?

C: Oh, I understand it. It said it's protecting me because I can't say no—especially to men.

Th: Well, did you know that before?

C: No. No, I had no idea. Actually, because of the headaches, I've never even had to say "no."

Th: Well, then, it's done a very effective job, hasn't it?

C: Yeah, I guess so.

Th: Do you agree that its intention is positive? Do you want to be protected from the consequences of not being able to say "no" to men?

C: I'd rather just say "no."

Th: Could you?

C: Well . . . I think so.

Th: So, *you* think so; but *that* part of you apparently doesn't agree.

C: Well, actually, I really do have trouble saying "no" to people —especially men.

Th: So, perhaps you do need that protection, at least until you learn how to say no.

C: Yeah, I do need it. Before I got the headaches, I, uh, got myself into a lot of trouble. I agree it has a good intention.

Th: You just don't like the way it's been satisfying that intention, right?

C: Yes.

Th: Until you're adept at saying "no" when it's necessary, would you like to continue to be protected from the consequences of not being able to say "no"?

C: Yes.

Th: Go inside and thank that part of you for having protected you these past years.

C: Okay (goes inside).

Th: Now, do you have a part of you that you consider to be your creative part?

C: Yeah, yeah I do.

Th: Good. I want you to go to your creative part and ask it if it would be willing to generate three other ways to satisfy the same intention while you're learning to say "no".

C: Okay. (Goes inside, smiles.) It says "yes."

Th: How did it say "yes"?

C: It spelled Y-E-S, in bright rainbow colors, just the way a creative part should.

Th: Great. Ask it to go ahead.

C: (Carol shuts her eyes and leans her head back. She nods once, twice, then three times.) Okay, I've got them.

Th: Do you want to tell me what they are?

C: Sure. One is only to be alone with men I want to say "yes" to. Two is to make myself ugly so he won't want me anyway. And three is to occupy him in activities that lead away from sex instead of toward it.

Th: Okay. Now, take those three new choices to the part that gives you headaches, and ask it if it agrees these will work at least as well as the headaches.

C: Okay. (Goes inside for several moments then her facial muscles contract.) Ouch! It says "yes".

Th: Good. Ask it if it will generate the new choices in the needed context.

C: (Goes inside; again facial contractions occur.) It says "yes".

Th: Ask it if there is any further need for giving you a headache.

C: (Goes inside; facial muscles remain relaxed.) Nothing happened.

Th: Great! So much for the headaches. Now, ask inside if any part objects to the negotiations that have taken place.

C: (Goes inside) Yes. I get a printout that says YES.

Th: Ask what the objection is.

C: It says in big, bold, block letters: LEARN TO SAY NO!

Th: I agree fully. Go inside and reassure that part that that's exactly what you are going to do, and since it has no trouble in raising an objection it can be very helpful in that process.

C: Okay. It says OKAY in big, bold, block letters.

Th: Good. Ask if there are any other objections to the negotiations that have taken place.

C: (Goes inside) Everything seems fine. I feel great.

Thus, Carol learned to identify an unwanted behavior (headaches) as a *way* of satisfying a positive intention ("staying out of trouble"). She established communication between her conscious verbal processes and the unconscious processes generating her symptom. In later sessions, I assisted Carol in accessing and organizing her responses to enable her to say "no" gracefully in appropriate contexts. Also, we employed reframing with other content so that the process itself could be integrated into her behavior. Soon she was able to do it on her own, making the need for a therapist unnecessary.

Often, sexual dysfunction is a manifestation of incongruity between conscious and unconscious behavioral processes. Reframing brings these processes into alignment by establishing a "meta" system that is directed toward the well being of the entire organism. The "meta" system is a verbalizing part that can contact and communicate with all other parts at the conscious or unconscious level. It does not take sides or label behavior or parts as "bad" or "sick." Instead it simply acts as a negotiator to bring various factions of an individual or a couple into alignment. In this way all of the inherent resources are utilized to achieve the goals agreed upon by the entire organism. (person or couple or family) Once all the steps of reframing are learned and integrated into a person's natural behavior he can accomplish any number of desired changes on his own.

Therapeutic Metaphor

A discussion of methods for evolving client systems from the present state to the desired state would be incomplete if it did not also offer an explanation of the use of therapeutic metaphor. Therapeutic metaphor being that special technique of storytelling which provides the client with important unconscious or conscious learnings and/or instigates in him new productive behaviors. Truly the art of therapeutic metaphor has been richly developed my Milton H. Erickson, M.D. He is a wizard at both the construction and delivery of therapeutic metaphors.

There are two books published by Meta Publications which concern themselves entirely with the full presentation of specific techniques for therapeutic metaphor construction. They are *The Patterns of Milton H. Erickson, M.D. Volume III*, by Bandler, Cameron-Bandler, De Lozier, and Grinder and *Therapeutic Metaphors*, by David Gordon. If the following presentation is intriguing to you I recommend reading these books.

Here I would like to offer just the barest essentials of metaphor construction with a few examples so that you can understand the general process and develop your own skills in this area. To quote from *Patterns III*

. . . The metaphor model concerns itself primarily with the techniques of creating metaphor through the use of verbal patterning. . . . The task defined by metaphor model II is to create a metaphor which has the following characteristics:

(a) it is an effective pace or description of the problem or situation which the client desires to have new choices about. The metaphor is an effective pace if the client's unconscious mind accepts the metaphor as being isomorphic (having a one to one relation in structure) with the problem or situation he wishes to have more choices about without an explicit awareness on the part of the client's conscious mind that the metaphor is intended to be isomorphic.

(b) it contains a solution or set of solutions which instruct the client's unconscious mind in specific techniques to generate new choices regarding the situation or problem they came for help with, without the client's conscious mind being aware that the metaphor is intended to provide a solution.

Any metaphor which has the two characteristics listed will have an impact therapeutically; We now will present techniques for the construction of such metaphors. The construction of therapeutically effective metaphor always involves the following three components;

(1) a problem or situation which the metaphor will be iso-morphic to
(2) the metaphor itself
(3) the specific procedures which the person creating the meta-phor will use to go from the problem or situation to meta-phor.[1]

While *Patterns III* provides a complete and explicit presentation concerning how to construct therapeutic metaphors, the following case history is a pertinent example of the use of metaphor in the context assisting a client to accomplish personal change.

An attractive woman named Dot came for counseling. She wanted help in learning to control her promiscuous behavior. She was married to a fine man (her description) and had two lovely children but participated in extra-marital relations whenever and with whomever possible. She wanted to stop this behavior. I used the following elements of her description to create a therapeutic metaphor. Like so many attractive women today Dot was also con-cerned about being overweight (which she was not) and so I used that content to make the metaphor appear like a more natural extension of our therapeutic interaction.

Problem Description	*Therapeutic Metaphor*
Dot's promiscuity is leading her to losing her husband and her self respect.	A woman on her way to obesity
Dot cannot resist the tempta-tion of other men	A woman who cannot resist gooey desserts and rich food when eating out.
Dot finds extra-marital sex more exciting.	This woman loves to eat out.
Dot is unsatisfied with her mari-tal sex relations	This woman merely picks at her own homecooked food.
Each extra-marital experience produces more guilt and brings	Each eating out experience pro-duces more fat.

her closer to losing her husband.

Dot's guilt becomes so painful she *had* to do something about it. She cannot sleep nights etc.	The fat lady had to do something about her habits. She could no longer fit into any of her clothes.
Dot had never developed satisfying sexual behaviors with her husband.	The fat lady had never learned to cook pleasing food for herself.

Each of the elements in the constructed metaphor so far are isomorphic (that is they are a one to one relationship in structure) to the presented problem. They pace the presented problem in that the form of each is the same. The next step is to move from pacing the problem to leading to a behavioral solution.

The desired response the metaphor is after is for Dot to change her behavior such that there is problem resolution. The story must then somehow provide for an appropriate behavior change from the obese woman since she represents Dot metaphorically.

Problem Solution	*Metaphorical Solution*
For Dot to apply energy to developing stimulating and satisfying sexual experiences with her husband.	The woman applied herself to rearranging the kitchen. She Began reading cookbooks to decide upon desirable dishes and began experimenting with creating healthy and satisfying meals
For Dot to find necessary satisfaction at home.	Over time, more quickly than you think, she found there was nothing in restaurants that could compare with her own home creations and she lost the desire to gorge herself elsewhere finding satisfaction at home.

For Dot to take pride in her marital relationship as well as finding sexual satisfaction with her husband.	Now slim this once fat woman takes great pride in her culinary skills as well as in her trim figure.

These then are the elements of a therapeutic metaphor designed to elicit a specific outcome. Anchoring and various other nonverbal as well as verbal techniques are utilized in this process of storytelling which help make it work. Other examples follow.

A couple, Don and Iris, sought marital counseling to improve a relationship that had been deteriorating for some time. Don was six years older than Iris. They had been married for six years and had two children, ages four and two. Although Iris had been a slim, attractive woman during their courtship, she had gained about fifty pounds since then. This weight was gained during each of her pregnancies and had not been taken off afterward. Don found her appearance to be disgusting and had not initiated sexual contact with her for several months. Since he worked in a management position with a large firm, there were some social commitments that went along with his job. He chose to deceive Iris about these, preferring to attend such functions alone, rather than risk embarrassment about her appearance.

It was Don who had made the decision to have children, and he had convinced Iris that it would be a good idea for them. But, as she gained weight during her first pregnancy Don began working overtime more and more. Even at the time of counseling, Iris' weight fluctuations were directly representative of how much time Don spent with her, and her overeating binges occured on evenings when he was away "working overtime." Although it was not evident that he was having, or had ever had, an affair, it was obvious the thought had certainly crossed his mind.

Don was meticulous about his appearance and talked about how he "saw himself." Iris, on the other hand, talked about how her life was empty and how she "needed something to fill it up." Don is highly visual; Iris is primarily kinesthetic. They were both congruent about loving each other, although Don almost visibly shuddered when he would look at Iris. Both described their previous sexual experience together as "idyllic." With two small children at home, Iris was extremely dependent upon Don for everything beyond her mothering role.

For both Don and Iris, the desired state was for her to lose weight, thus reviving his physical desire for her. For Iris, Don's desire (or, lack of it) very much controled the condition of her subjective experience. The more he moved away from her, the more she ate to fill the empty aching within her and, resulting from this, the further he would move away.

Since an increase in Don's attentiveness towards Iris would have greatly facilitated her weight loss, improving her overall happiness and self-esteem as well, I might have simply told him how his actions worked and depended on his good intentions to remedy the problem. But the good intentions he had were not succeeding. Somehow, his experience of being with Iris, as she was, needed to be enhanced. I was certain that if Don could be warmly supportive of Iris, even protective, she would respond by losing weight and by "being more her own person" (her own words). However, her present appearance prevented either of them from eliciting the desired response from the other.

Therefore, keeping in mind both the short-term goal of increasing Don's attentiveness towards Iris as well as the more long-term goal of strengthening a mutually-nourishing relationship, I decided to use therapeutic metaphor with them. In constructing it, I utilized information gathered from them concerning their behavior and incorporated specific verbal expressions used by Don to make it yet more effective.

So, in the metaphor designed for Don and Iris, which follows, Don is cast as "Uncle Ronnie" while the "land" and the "artichoke plants" represent Iris. The basic relationship of a farmer who nurtures and elicits a response from the land is kept constant throughout. Metaphorically, this relationship is congruent with Don and Iris's relationship. The story was told as follows:

"You say your father was a rancher of sorts. My Uncle Ronnie is a rancher; I mean, that's what they're called in California, no matter what they grow. He wasn't always a rancher, though. No, before that he had a career in business and he was good at it, too. Real up and coming fellow. But his dad—my granddad— had this big, beautiful piece of land out on the coast of California. Well, Ronnie knew someday it would probably all be his. He kept an eye on it as time went by.

"But his business career took a lot of his time. You know how that is. Finally, the time came when his father called him out to California and told him things were just too heavy for him and that he needed Ronnie to take things over. The way it looked to Ronnie was that this could be a great opportunity. Financially, he could make something of the place and it was such a beautiful piece of land—he couldn't resist.

"For awhile he simply enjoyed his new position as a gentleman rancher. But then he decided it was time to get down to business. His father had grown mostly crops of cut flowers. Very beautiful. But not that productive to Ronnie's way of thinking. After investigating various possibilities, he decided that growing artichokes (having babies) would be the better use of the land. They were hardy, perfect for the climate, considered a delicacy of sorts, and got a high price.

"So, he had the fields of flowers plowed under and sowed seeds for artichoke plants. He felt this was a wise and prodigious move on his part. But artichoke plants take some time before they really produce and Ronnie was an impatient man. His interest began to wander. One day as he looked out over the fields, they seemed quite ugly to him. He would tell himself that this was more practical, but still he missed the lovely flowers. More and more, he stayed away from the land and left the tending to others. Of course, the land suffered. The hired hands didn't care as much for the land; after all, it wasn't theirs. And the land showed the results of Ronnie's neglect.

"Ronnie told me that one day he went out to the fields and looked around. He was appalled by the lumpy mounds and the unattractive artichoke plants, their leaves sticking out all over. He said to himself, 'My God, what have I done? This is awful. I don't even want to call it my own. I should have left it alone. I wish I'd never touched it.'

"But, he had. And what was he to do with it now? True, it was now producing artichokes and there was a good market for artichokes. But the land needed more of his own personal tending and attention if it was going to be really productive. Deep down inside, he knew this was true.

"As he walked back to the main house, he reached out and picked an artichoke, carrying it with him. While sitting at the kitchen table pondering his problems, he began to really study that artichoke. It was kind of ugly. All those bulging, inedible leaves on the outside. He found himself wondering why anybody would be tempted by such a thing.

"But then he began to gently peel the artichoke. And, as each layer came off, he became more and more enthralled with what lay underneath. Why, it was beautiful! The smooth, tender inside leaves led him to the heart of the artichoke. Of course, that's what tempted people to buy and to grow artichokes. They knew about the lovely and succulent heart that lay within.

"As he now looked out the window, he began to see a sea of artichoke hearts across his fields. He laughed because, instead of a lot of ugly lumpy sticky plants, he could now see a lot of plants working very hard with all those outer layers protecting the precious inner heart which, after all, is what everyone wanted of them. Those thick, spiney outer layers kept the heart of the artichoke from anyone who wasn't willing to take the time to get at the treasure inside.

"Something about this touched Ronnie, for he appreciated the idea of being vulnerable. And what's more, the artichoke couldn't peel itself. It couldn't expose its inner treasure without him. These were his fields, his plants, and he suddenly felt the strong desire to tend and care for them, to insure their growth and productivity. He would make sure that the plants and the fruit were cared for tenderly lest the precious heart be bruised.

"Now, of course, my Uncle Ronnie is tremendously successful as a rancher and is very proud of his land and what it bears. He says of the early days that he nearly lost sight of where he was going because he let himself wander when things weren't looking good. And that wandering cost him the extra time and trouble it took to bring things back into shape.

"Once he took a closer look at what he had, he gladly gave all he had to offer rather than take a chance on losing everything he'd always wanted. Naturally, the land responded by making him a very rich and proud man. Everyone could see he had something of value."

This metaphor worked very well to elicit the desired responses. Don became more attentive to Iris. He began to encourage and even participate in a weight loss program with her. His words were that he had an investment in his marriage and he would have to put some time and energy into it if that investment were going to pay off.

The special advantage of metaphors is that people respond without *trying*. Their conscious processes do not interfere and, while knowing that something happened, they really are not sure just what or how it happened.

Had I chosen a different desired outcome, the metaphor would have been constructed differently. If the desired response was for Iris to become more assertive and independent, the metaphor might have had the land go wild from neglect, becoming overrun with strange and beautiful plants such that Uncle Ronnie no longer knew his way through his own land: "And it was like a virgin frontier to be discovered and perhaps tamed and cultivated once again. But, alas, the land would have none of his taming and cultivating, for it had outgrown him and, if anything would instead tame and cultivate him to suit its own needs."

Such a metaphor would certainly have elicited a different outcome than the previous one. It was my opinion that a really assertive and independent response from Iris, at this time, would have been destructive to their relationship rather than beneficial. This opinion guided my behavior in constructing a metaphor that would elicit a *useful response*. When using metaphor do be sure to keep the desired outcome firmly in mind throughout both the construction and telling of the metaphor.

The following excerpts from therapy transcripts further demonstrate the effective use of therapeutic metaphor:

"Case History: Bud"

Bud was suffering from impotency. He had no history of erections sufficient for coitus nor of ejaculation. At age fourteen, he was seduced by his aunt who lived with him and his mother. This aunt repeatedly humiliated him because of his inability to perform. There had been no father in the home since Bud was twelve and the sexual incidents were never revealed to his mother. Although Bud had been married six months, the marriage remained unconsummated. His description of his wife matches that of his aunt to a tee, but Bud gives no indication of being consciously aware of this similarity. He has pictures of both his wife and aunt in his wallet and even the physical similarities are striking. His aunt is now dead.

The metaphor was constructed using these components:

Bud = Fireman (Bud is in fact a fireman)
penis = fire hose
unconscious control = hydrant
burning church = his Aunt
building next door = his wife

"My mother told me a story that her sister had heard from a neighbor in Wichita, Kansas concerning a fire. It seems the town's largest and most important church had caught fire. No one knew how it had started, but the firemen were summoned to put it out. Upon arrival, it was plain to see she was ablaze from bottom to top. And the heat she put out! The firemen were irregulars, not well trained, and scared as hell. Seems all the regulars were away at the annual firemens' picnic. Untrained as they were, the firemen did their level best but hardly knew where to begin. With a great sense of urgency, they hooked their hose to the hydrant, uncoiled it, and approached the burning church. It was their intention to enter once the hose was working and to save what they could.

"But, alas, no water filled the hose and they dared not enter without it. You, being a fireman can imagine how frustrating this was. The firemen grew desperate and frantic, wasting time with their frenzy while the church burned away.

"It was only when they had accepted defeat and had turned away that the needed actions became obvious. Approaching the hydrant with curiosity, the frenzy gone because the church could not even hope to be saved, the firemen easily found the way to open the valve releasing water long held under pressure in the hose. But, damnit, it had come too late. . . .

However as they turned back to watch the church crumble into dying coals they noticed that the house next to the church, had caught fire by flying sparks and embers—and there was life inside it. (The church was gone there was nothing to be gained by directing efforts there.) And upon hearing the cries of those inside the house the firemen rushed with their hose to quench the thirsty flames. Entering with the hose at full power, they thoroughly put out the blaze, leaving not even a tendril of flame to flicker on.

They were tired and satisfied firemen as they withdrew from the house. All of the lives had been saved, and the only sign left of the fire were the smoky sighs escaping through open windows.

The church had burned to the ground, but even the regular fire-fighters had agreed that she was beyond saving, even from the beginning and, they had been right to attend to the house next door. Before leaving though, the firemen checked the hydrant once more, making sure all connections were as they should be. . . . in case they ever needed to come again."

"Case History: Allen"

Several years ago in a training seminar, a young man, Allen, pleaded for help with a very personal problem. Though I told him that the training seminar was not the place to seek private consultation, his insistent and persevering pleas induced me to give him a few private moments.

His very urgent and pressing problem was that of premature ejaculation. He had suffered from this for several years without previously seeking help for it. But now he was in love, truly in love, and it was terribly important that he be a great lover for his new woman. Because of my knowledge of Allen's conscious and unconscious behavior in the context of the ongoing training seminar— and also because the evening's subject would be hypnotic metaphor—I decided to use just that as a therapeutic intervention with him.

To his conscious mind, I merely consoled him, saying that not much could be done for premature ejaculation. My suggestion was to reframe the behavior toward his new woman, telling him to say she was so enticing, so exciting, that he simply couldn't control himself; that his premature ejaculations were just a response to her sexual prowess. Allen was stunned by this suggestion, but politely accepted it, and he even began to plan just how he would phrase his post-coital remarks.

During the evening training session, I induced an adequate deep-trance state in Allen and told him several stories, all of which were constructed to elicit a specific response. One story, which exemplifies the others, follows. I'm sure the intended response will be obvious to the reader, although it was not at all obvious to those in the training seminar. In fact, the majority of those in attendance believed it to be a trance induction with the desired response being a deep trance state.

"There are many ways to go many places. For the man who has worked hard all year there is but a brief two-week vacation. A brief two weeks in which he must cram all the vacation pleasure of a year. What frustration to cram a year's pleasure into two weeks! Often he might pick a destination to reach in order that he might spend his vacation time there. Once picked, he might locate the destination on a map and, on that map, he might choose the quickest route possible to reach his chosen destination. He might even find a shortcut, so much does he desire to reach his chosen destination. And that might be all very well.

"*But* that is how he spends all of his life. By deciding where it is that he is going and taking the shortest possible route in getting there. What of others who may wish to journey with him? What of the unforeseen adventures and delights ignored by setting his sights only upon the destination point? And this man, this man would even take the same shortcut to the same destination year after year. That is, until one year.

And a good thing too. That year a friend was going to that same destination point. The Grand Canyon. That's where they were both going. And that's where they both had been. But the friend drove. And the friend was in no hurry to get there. The friend did not even have a roadmap or a route, but nonetheless was completely sure of arriving at the desired place and was content to take all the time in the world to get there.

"At first, the man was impatient. But then he became intrigued and even beguiled with what this very odd way of traveling had to offer. For they did whatever fancied them at the moment. They took sidetrips where they were surprised and delighted with what they found.

"And no matter where they went, the closer they came to the Grand Canyon. Sometimes when a sidetrip would be especially delightful to the man, he wouldn't want to leave. And his friend would persuade him to move on by reminding him, "You can come again and again to a favorite place. And you can leave it, knowing you can come again whenever you like." Only then would the man move on. They were both surprised when they reached the Grand Canyon itself. So engrossed were they in each phase of their journey, their arrival was an unexpected extra pleasure.

"His friend traced the way they had come in the warm earth: "You can come this way and you can come that way or that way. There are as many ways to get there as there are pleasures to have. They can all take you there. Some quickly, some slowly. It matters not. It only matters to be where you are when you are there, instead of where you are going before you get there. When you are where you are, nothing will be missed."

"And, year after year, the friend and he traveled to places known and unknown, and they did so comfortably and with great pleasure."

This metaphor proved to be effectual in altering Allen's sexual behavior. He later reported having no difficulty with premature ejaculations over the next several weeks. His learning behavior also changed in response to this metaphor so that, rather than using methods he was well acquainted with, he began to explore various phases of the processes we were working with in the seminar. As he did so, his enjoyment increased along with the expression of his creativity.

Allen was never consciously aware of any sex therapy taking place. When next I saw him he smugly remarked that there had been no need to worry; he had found other ways around the problem. I replied that I believed him absolutely. He paused, looked at me out of the corner of his eye, began to speak, then checked himself, shrugged his shoulders and said, "Feels good, you know."

Notes

1. R Bandler, J Grinder, L. Cameron-Bandler, J Dehozier, *Patterns of the Hypnotic Techniques of Milton H. Erickson, M.D. Volume III* (Cupertino Ca: Meta Publications, 1979) pg 32

Part IV

Futurepacing

Although futurepacing is an integral aspect of all the aforementioned techniques, it merits special emphasis because of its practical as well as theoretical importance. Essentially, futurepacing refers to the process of ensuring that the changes accomplished during therapy become generalized and available in the appropriate outside contexts. Too often, changes that occur in therapy remain anchored to the therapist's office or even to the therapist himself rather than being available to the client in the specific situations that most need the new behaviors and responses.

The primary method of futurepacing new behaviors is by anchoring the new behavior or response to a sensory stimulus that naturally occurs in the applicable context. Step five of "reframing" futurepaces new behaviors by asking a part to take responsibility for generating those new behaviors in the appropriate context. As in the "reframing" example with Tom I asked him how he would know when he needed the new choices. For him the signal was feeling "pushed" so I anchored the new behavioral choices to that feeling. In "changing history" futurepacing is accomplished by asking the client in what future circumstance will they again need that resource which you have worked with them to access and to alter their subjective experience of their past. When the future circumstance is identified the client is then to generate an internal projection of that circumstance in which that needed resource is available and expressed. In this way the resource becomes attached to the context in which it is needed (futurepacing). The therapeutic metaphor futurepaces by including leading or future behaviors as a part of its construct. The futurepacing of those changes accomplished with visual-kinesthetic-disassociation is best done by presenting the client with the actual stimulus which previously triggered the phobic response. So if it was of heights to take them to a high place and learn if the desired change has been accomplished.

Futurepacing can be done very directly. One way is to ask the client, "What is the very first thing you will see, hear or feel externally that will indicate you need this resource?" When the specific experience is identified have the client generate it internally and then anchor it to the appropriate resource. Then when the stimulus occurs in external experience it can naturally or unconsciously trigger the appropriate feelings/behavior. For instance, anchoring feelings of passion (the resource) to the feeling of smooth cool sheets or the sound of his name softly whispered or the sight of a yellow rose is futurepacing the resource of passionate feelings to specific externally occurring experiences. This process can be done with couples by anchoring the new, more useful behaviors/-responses to phenomena that already naturally occur; For example, how he scratches his head, the sight of their front door, the sound of the television being turned off. Any of these can serve as triggers for initiating some newly acquired behavioral choice on the part of clients. Role playing can often serve to futurepace changes also. But most preferable of all is to present the client with the actual situation in which new behaviors/choices need to be expressed. While usually impossible when dealing with sexual dysfunction this is still the best way of testing your work and insuring the full integration of new behaviors.

What is most important about futurepacing is to do it, and not just leave it to the client's conscious mind to take the accomplishments of a session into their ongoing lives. Although the conscious mind may try very hard, it usually recalls the new behavior only after it has already failed by exhibiting the former behavior. Unconscious processes however, work automatically. So, it is the therapist's task to implant the new choices at the unconscious level, making sure that the triggers for these new more useful behavioral choices will work and that they are certain of occurring at the appropriate time.

Futurepacing is not frosting on the therapy cake. Without adequate futurepacing the accomplishments of a session are often lost. It is the final step in any effective therapeutic intervention.

Part V

Conclusion

I believe that the information contained in this presentation is useful both to the seasoned clinical practitioner and to the developing therapist still in training. It provides new and useful ways of understanding verbal and nonverbal communication. Throughout I have presented to you many of my own methods and style of doing therapy. The structure upon which I hinge my own methods and style consists of the three aforementioned steps; (1) gathering information and establishing rapport (2) evolving the client from their present state to their desired state and (3) futurepacing. To summarize the activities involved in each of these:

The initial step of gathering information includes determining the client's representational system, lead system, and the naturally-occurring anchors that trigger the sequence of internal and external processes that constitute the client's present state and desired state. This information is gathered in the form of verbal descriptions as well as by observing the client's behavior in the therapeutic context. You use your well-trained ears and eyes to gather this information from the sensory experience that each client presents. The Meta-model serves as a linguistic tool for gathering the most complete verbal description possible of the present state and the desired state.

Once you have gathered all the information necessary to understand how the present system works and what the desired state is, a therapeutic intervention is chosen that will result in the client's experiencing the desired state. The therapist then evolves the client system to the desired state by employing a chosen technique or integration of techniques. The methods offered here—overlap, anchoring, change history, visual-kinesthetic disassociation, re-framing, and metaphor—are but a sampling of possibilities.

When the desired state has been accomplished, the task is to consolidate and integrate changes so they can become generalized into the client's ongoing behavior. This futurepacing ensures the perpetuation of the desired-state experience. The process of generalization occurs by making sure that the new behaviors or responses are triggered by the appropriate contextual sensory experience.

To utilize this theoretical framecork and the various methods presented there are two necessary ingredients that the individual therapist must bring into play for this or any other model to be used effectively. As stated earlier these two ingredients are flexibility of behavior and sensory experience.

Flexibility of behavior refers to having choices in communication style as well as choices in methods of intervention. This presentation has offered numerous choices in techniques and methods of intervention, but *how* they are done is as important as doing them. As professional communicators, it is essential for therapists to have an infinite variety of behaviors available *to them at all times.* We should consider resistance on the part of a client to be a comment on our own behavior, not the client's. It is our job to be able to pace adequately the client's model of the world and then to elicit responses that bypass resistance. This requires flexibility on our part to be able to match the client's behavior and to use aspects of his own behavior and ours to elicit useful responses.

The importance of a therapist's ability to verbalize in a manner that is understandable to the client, regardless of cultural or educational background, is accepted. However, even this is lost if the therapist lacks the sensory experience to know by his client's responses whether or not he is indeed being understood. It cannot be emphasized too strongly: the therapist must be able to vary all the aspects of his communication and to use his sensory experience to know whether the manner and style being employed is appropriate for eliciting the desired response from the client.

When assisting clients in making changes, it is often necessary to elicit from them a wide range of responses. Of first order is to acquire the client's trust and confidence. Once acquired, it may be necessary to induce anything from overt anger to abject hopelessness, from deep sympathy to wild joy, in order to accomplish the therapeutic goal. As such while it is essential that the therapist be able to vary his behavior widely to elicit the desired responses he must use the sensory feedback he receives in making adjustments

in his behavior necessary to achieve success. Thus keeping in mind
the effect each of our verbal and nonverbal communications has on
others, the effective therapist will construct his communications in
relationship to the responses he wishes to elicit. When sensory
experience tells him he is not getting the desired response, he
varies aspects subtly or dramatically until his sensory experience
indicates success.

Those therapists recognized as being genius in stature certainly
display wide variability in their behaviors. Especially useful examples of the range of Milton Erickson's behavior can be found in
Haley's *Uncommon Therapy*[1] and *Advanced Techniques of Hypnotherapy.*
[2] Lesser known, but no less effective, is Frank Farrelly whose
unique style is presented in his book *Provocative Therapy.*[3] Certainly, the therapeutic miracles that occur in the workshops con-
ducted by my esteemed colleagues Richard Bandler and John
Grinder exemplify their infinite flexibility of behavior and sensory
experience.

Possibly some might think of such tactics as manipulation. Well,
if manipulation is utilizing all available conscious and unconscious
skills to assist people in making changes that they certainly desire
to make, then manipulation it may be. Often, I have found it
necessary to jeopardize the positive feelings a client may have for
me in order to generate an experience that will be beneficial to his
or her process of change. But, even though I may seem manipula-
tive, coarse, even cruel at times, my highest priority is always the
client's well-being. Such well-being is not necessarily enhanced by
supportive or indulgent behavior on the part of the therapist. It's
more important for the client to change in the desired way than for
me to win a popularity contest. The client is in therapy not for my
benefit, but for his. With no limitations to behavior other than
physical violence and seduction, the therapist is free to explore
many avenues leading to productive change.

As with any new material, learning the patterns presented here
may at first seem a monumental undertaking. In a short period of
time, however, these patterns can become integrated into your
experience and you will be able to use them in a systematic way on
a largely unconscious level. Since they are content-free, you can
use them in any context and with anyone, being sure to season
them with your own personal style and finesse.

As you connect each person with the needed resource from

within themselves for their desired changes, you will indeed become richer yourself. The great trick is to discover what it is that keeps people tied to their limitations and then to undo the knots —perhaps one at a time, perhaps very quickly. It is a matter of recognizing that the future grows out of the here and now; and that people who are not free and eager for change will have nothing to do with inventing better futures for anyone.

The task is now before you, the reader, to glean from this text that which can be valuable to you, to integrate it into your behavior —enhancing it with your own personal style—and to use it to enrich both your own and your clients' future experiences. Do this remembering always that "there are no mistakes in communication, there are only *outcomes.*" You *do* have the choices needed to make happy endings come true.

Notes

1. J. Haley, *Uncommon Therapy* (NY; Grune and Stratton, 1968).
2. J. Haley, *Advanced Techniques of Hypnosis and Therapy: Selected Papers of Milton H. Erickson, M.D.,* (N.Y. Grune and Stratton 1967).
3. F. Farrelly and J. Brandsma, *Provocative Therapy* (Cupertino, Ca; Meta Publications 1978)

Appendix I

The Meta Model[1]

Throughout the text of this book I have referred you to this appendix for a presentation of the Meta-model. The Meta-model is an explicit set of linguistic information gathering tools designed to reconnect a person's language to the experience represented by their language.

Fundamental to the useful application of this material is the concept that language is *not* experience, but rather a *representation* of experience, like a map is a representation of a territory. While I'm sure that you are familiar with the notion that "the map is not the territory," I'm wondering if you have fully realized that, as human beings, we will forever experience only the map and not the territory. Actually, as persons who assist people in changing, this is to our advantage. We but alter maps; that is, we change people's subjective experience of the world, not the world.

We make our maps out of the interaction between internal and external experience. Because we humans represent or build maps of our experience with language, a set of tools like those provided by the Meta-model becomes invaluable. Essentially the Meta-model serves as an interface between language and experience.

All of the proceeding material was developed by Richard Bandler and John Grinder, and a more detailed presentation can be found in *The Structure of Magic, Volume I.* What follows is a summation of their material, reorganized to best facilitate its usefulness to you, the reader.

Three Universal Modeling Processes

Because we do not operate directly on the world we live in, we create models or maps of the world which we use to guide our behavior. As an effective therapist, it is crucial to understand the client's model or map of the world. Human behavior, no matter how bizarre or resistant it may seem, makes sense when it is seen in the context of the choices generated by a person's map or model. These models we create guide us and allow us to make sense out of our experience. They are not to be evaluated in terms of good, bad, healthy, sick, or crazy, but rather in terms of their ability to be useful: Useful in making it possible to cope successfully and respond creatively to the world around us. It is not that our clients are making the wrong choices, but that they do not have enough choices available when needed. Each of us makes the very best choice available to us from our model of the world. However, there is a surplus of impoverished models lacking in useful choices as evidenced by the abundancy of interpersonal and innerpersonal conflict. "It is not the world that lacks choices but the individual's model of the world," say Grinder and Bandler.

We create our models through three universal human modeling processes: Generalization, Deletion, and Distortion. These processes allow us to survive, grow, learn, understand, and experience the richness the world has to offer. But if we mistake our subjective reality for reality, these same processes limit us and squelch our abilities to do the former.

As stated by Bandler and Grinder, "Generalization is the process by which elements or pieces of a person's model become detached from their original experience and come to represent the entire category of which the experience is an example." We learn to function in the world by generalizing. A child learns to open a door by turning a knob. He then generalizes this experience to recognizing the many varieties of phenomena that fall within some set of limitations as "doors" and then attempts to open them by turning the knobs. As a man enters a darkened room he reaches for the light switch; he does not have to learn a new strategy for acquiring light in a room every time he desires it. However, the same process can work as a limitation. If a man fails once to perform sexually in a way that he deems adequate and therefore generalizes his experience to deciding that he was no good at sex, he would deny himself much indeed. Or if a woman decides that men are insensitive based on limited and selective experiences, she loses a great deal. Too, each of us makes an infinite number of generalizations that are useful and appropriate in some situations and not in others. A child learns from his family that crying and whining will get him what he wants, yet the same behavior will likely get him abuse from his peers. If he generalizes only the former and not the latter, he may not be able to generate more appropriate and useful behavior in the company of his peers. If a young man generalizes only those behaviors that win the respect of his fellow males, he may experience great difficulty in obtaining respect and interest from women. Whether or not a generalization is useful must be evaluated within a particular context.

"A second mechanism which we can use to cope effectively or to defeat ourselves is Deletion. Deletion is a process by which we selectively pay attention to certain dimensions of our experience and exclude others" (Bandler and Grinder). This allows us to focus our awareness and attend to one portion of our experience over others. Thus, someone can read a book with people around him talking or with the TV on or records playing. This process makes coping possible and allows us to not be overwhelmed by external stimuli. Again though, the same process can be limiting if we delete portions of our experience that are necessary for a full and rich model of the world. The adolescent who believes he is being unjustly treated and picked on without including his own participation in bringing the situation into existence has not developed a useful model of the world. A therapist who deletes from his or her experience evidence of boredom in the session is limiting their own experience as well as that of their clients.

"The third modeling process is that of distortion. Distortion is the process which allows us to make shifts in our experience of sensory data" (Bandler and Grinder). Without this process we could not plan for the future or make dreams into reality. We misrepresent reality in fiction, art, and even science. A microscope, a novel, and a painting are all examples of our ability to distort and make misrepresentations of reality. We can limit ourselves with distortion in many ways. Think, for example, of the person who distorts all critical messages with the response "I'm unlovable." As a result of such distortion, any value in the criticisms is lost and possibly the opportunities for change and growth as well. Or consider the frequent distortion of turning a process into a "thing." When "relationship" is disassociated from the process of relating, those involved suffer a loss. It becomes something "out there" to be talked about, out of control, no longer dynamic.

Because these three universal modeling processes are expressed in language patterns we can use that set of linguistic tools known as the meta model to challenge them when they are found to limit rather than expand a person's behavioral choices.

The Meta-model accomplishes this by assisting clients and the therapist in the process of reconnecting the client's language to the experience that is represented by it. It is a set of tools derived from those patterns in human language and, as such, it is a set of tools useful in any human endeavor involving language.

The Meta-model is designed to teach the listener how to hear and respond to the *form* of the speaker's communication. The content may vary infinitely, but the form of the information given allows the listener the opportunity to respond in such a way as to obtain the fullest meaning from the communication. With the Meta-model it is possible to quickly discern the richness and the limits of the information given as well as the human modeling processes used by the speaker. Listening and responding in terms of the Meta-model distinctions allows the most to be achieved in understanding and learning from any specific communication.

The Meta-model distinctions fall into three natural groupings:

Gathering Information
Limits of the Speaker's Model
Semantic Ill-formedness

Gathering information refers to gaining, through appropriate questions and responses, an accurate and full description of the content being presented. Again, this process assists in reconnecting the speaker's language with his or her experience. There are four distinctions in this category:

Deletion
Lack of Referential Index
Unspecified Verbs
Nominalizations

"Deletion"

Recognizing when a deletion has occurred and assisting in recovering the deleted information aids in restoring a fuller representation of the experience. To recover the missing material, the meta-modeler asks: ABOUT WHOM? or ABOUT WHAT? For example,

"I don't understand."
(response) "You don't understand *what?*"
(or) "*What* don't you understand?"

"I'm afraid"
(response) "*What* or *whom* are you afraid of?"
"I don't like him."
(response) "*What about* him don't you like?"

"He's the best."
(response) "He's the best *what?*"

"He's the best listener."
(response) "He's the best listener *amongst whom?*"
(or) "*Between whom*"

In the case of deletion, asking the question, "How, specifically?" will give information concerning the representational system being used by the client.

"I don't understand."
(response) "How, specifically, do you know you don't understand?"
"It's just not *clear* to me." (i.e., visual rep.)

"Lack of Referential Index"

Lack of referential index is a case of generalization that limits a person's model of the world by leaving out the detail and richness necessary to have a variety of options for coping. With this process a person takes an experience and generalizes it in such a way that it's totally out of perspective or out of proportion. To challenge a lack of referential index, ask: WHO SPECIFICALLY? or WHAT SPECIFICALLY?

"No one wants me."
(response) "*Who, specifically,* doesn't want you?"

"They are obstinate."
(response) "*Who, specifically,* is obstinate?"

"This is hard."
(response) *"What, specifically,* about this is hard for you?"

"Unspecified Verbs"

Unspecified verbs leave us in the dark about clearly understanding the experience being described. All verbs are relatively unspecified. However, "kiss" is much more specific than "touch." If someone says he's been hurt, it could have been from a harsh look given by someone important to them, or they might have been hit by a car. Asking for verb specification reconnects the person more fully to his or her experience. To challenge unspecified verbs, ask: HOW SPECIFICALLY?

"He rejected me."
(response) *"How, specifically,* did he reject you?"

"They ignored me."
(response) *"How, specifically,* did they ignore you?"

"The children force me to punish them."
(response) *"How, specifically,* do the children force you to punish them?"

"Nominalizations"

Nominalizations are those words that have transformed from process words (verbs) into nouns. As such, an ongoing process becomes a thing or an event. When this happens, we lose choices and there is a need to be reconnected with the ongoing dynamic processes of life. Quoting Bandler and Grinder, "Specifically reversing nominalizations assists the person in coming to see that what he had considered an event finished and beyond his control is a continuing process which can be changed." Nominalizations can be distinguished from regular nouns in several ways. For those who enjoy visualizing, make a picture of a wheelbarrow in your mind's eye. Now put a chair, then a cat, then your mother in the wheelbarrow. Now try putting failure, virtue, projection, statement, and confusion into that wheelbarrow. As you can see, nominalizations are not persons, places or things that can be put into a wheelbarrow. Another way to test for nominalizations is to check whether the event word fits into the blank syntactic frame, "an ongoing _____:"

an ongoing *problem*   nominalization
an ongoing *elephant*
an ongoing *chair*
an ongoing *relationship*   nominalization

To transform a nominalization back into a process word, use it as a verb in the response:

"I don't get any recognition."
(response) "How would you like to be recognized?"

"Pay attention."
(response) "What do you want me to attend to?"

"I regret my decision."
(response) "Does anything stop you from re-deciding?"

"I want help."
(response) "How do you want to be helped?"

The next grouping is referred to as "Limits" of the speaker's model. These distinctions identify the limits and by challenging them appropriately, you can assist *a person* in enriching his model of the world by expanding it. The two distinctions in this category are:

Universal Quantifiers
Modal Operators (primarily, modal operators of necessity)

"Universal Quantifiers"

Universal quantifiers refer to the set of words typified by "all," "every," "always," "never," "every," "nobody." Emphasizing the generalization described by the speaker's universal quantifiers by exaggerating it—both by voice quality and by inserting additional universal quantifiers—serves to challenge them. Challenging the speaker's universal quantifiers assists him in finding the exception to his generalization and thus having more choices. Another way to challenge directly is to ask whether the speaker has had an experience that contradicts his own generalization.

"I never do anything right."
(response) "You *absolutely never ever* do *anything* right?"
(or) "Have you *ever* done *anything* right?"

"You're always lying to me."
(response) "I'm *always* lying to you?"

"It's impossible to get what I want."
(response) "Have you *ever* gotten something you wanted?"

"Modal Operators of Necessity"

Modal operators of necessity refer to those words which indicate there are no choices: "have to," "must," "can't," "It's necessary." Challenging these modal operators takes a person beyond the limits they have heretofore accepted. There are two excellent responses that serve to challenge these limits: WHAT STOPS YOU? and WHAT WOULD HAPPEN IF YOU DID? The response "What stops you?" serves to take the person into the past to find from what experience this generalization was formed. "What would happen if you did?" demands that the client go into the future and imagine possible consequences. The importance of these responses in assisting someone to achieve a richer and fuller model of the world is to be greatly emphasized.

"I can't do it."
(response) "What stops you?"

"You have to finish by Tuesday."
(response) "What would happen if I didn't?"

"I have to take care of other people."
(response) "What will happen if you don't?"

"I can't tell him the truth."
(response) "What will happen if you do?"
(or) "What stops you from telling him the truth?"

The third distinction of the meta model is concerned with semantic ill-formedness. "The purpose of recognizing sentences which are semantically ill-formed is to assist the person in identifying the portions of his model which are distorted in some way that impoverishes the experiences which are available to him" (Bandler and Grinder). By changing those portions of his model that are semantically ill-formed, a person achieves greater choices and freedom in operating upon the world. It is these portions which frequently stop the person from acting in ways he would otherwise choose to act. The three classes of semantic ill-formedness are:

Cause and Effect
Mind Reading
Lost Performative

"Cause and Effect"

Cause and effect involves the belief that some action on the part of one person can cause another person to experience some emotion or inner state. As such, the person responding experiences himself as having no choice concerning how to respond. When this is challenged, it allows the person to explore and question whether the causal connection is indeed true. He can then begin to wonder what other choices he can generate for responding. The challenge is one of asking: *"How* does X cause Y?"

"Your writing on the wall bothers me."
(response) "How does my writing on the wall bother you?"
(or ". . . make you feel bothered?")

"You frustrate me."
(response) How do I frustrate you? "How is it possible for me to frustrate you?"
(or, ". . . make you feel frustrated?")

"His ideas annoy me."
(response) "How do his ideas annoy you?"
(or, ". . . make you feel annoyed?")

"I'm sad because you're late."
(response) "How does my being late make you feel sad?"

"Mind Reading"

Mind reading refers to the belief on the part of the speaker that one person can know what another is thinking or feeling without a direct communication from the second person. In other words, this is a way to recognize when someone is acting on delusions rather than information. Obviously, mind reading can do much to inhibit the usefulness of a person's model of the world. The listener responds to mind reading by asking: "How, specifically, do you know X?" This provides a way for the speaker to become aware of and even to question those assumptions he may have previously taken for granted.

"Everybody thinks I'm taking too much time."
(response) "How, specifically, do you know what everybody is thinking?"

"I'm sure you can see how I feel?"
(response) "How, specifically, can you be sure I see how you feel?"

"I know what's best for him."
(response) "How do you know what is best for him?"

"He never considers the consequences."
(response) "How, specifically, do you know he never considers the consequences?"

"Lost Performative"

The lost performative refers to those statements that are in the form of a generalization about the world itself rather than a statement recognized as belonging to the speaker's model of the world. Usually these are judgments. The speaker is using the lost performative when he takes rules that are appropriate to him and his model of the world and puts them on others. Phrased in the vernacular, this is called "laying your trip on somebody else." The purpose in challenging this is to assist the speaker to own comfortably his own rules and opinions while allowing the rest of the world to have its own. Frequently, with lost performative, there is no indication that the speaker is even aware of other options or possibilities. To challenge lost performative, ask: FOR WHOM?

"It wrong to be on welfare."
(response) "It's wrong *for whom* to be on welfare?"

"This is the right way to do it."
(response) "This is the right way *for whom* to do it?"

"That's a sick thing to do."
(response) "Sick *for whom?*"

Thus the Meta-model asks the questions What, How, Who in response to the specific form of the speaker's language.

As stated at the beginning, the Meta-model is a set of tools and better communication can be built by using these tools. Your skills as a meta modeler depend on your willingness and ability to implement actively the questions and the responses provided by the Meta-model.

While practicing the Meta-model pay exquisite attention to your internal processes. Since it is a formalization of intuitive behavior, the Meta-model responses will occur at those times when you would have had to refer to an internally-generated experience in order to understand a client's communication. For example, when a client says, "My father hurt me," in order to understand fully what is meant by this statement, you must ask "How?" The client may have been beaten, yelled at, scowled at, or simply ignored. As a therapist, if you decide that you understand what is meant by the word "hurt" by calling simply on your own experience, then you are in fact meeting the client at *your* model of the world, not his.

The Meta-model is a set of tools that allows you to stay in "external sensory experience," getting information from the client, which then keeps you from going "inside," to internally, generated experience for understanding. While you are learning the Meta-model, the appropriate responses can be inserted at those points when you formerly would have had to refer to your own internal experience to understand (or attempt to understand) the client's meaning. The Meta-model asks that the client make his communication more clearly understandable; not that you fill in the missing pieces from your own subjective reality for him. When a client presents to you a verbal communication, for example, as "I'm afraid of crowds," if you—as a therapist—go inside and decide "Oh yeah, 'afraid of crowds,' yes, I know about that," then you have missed the opportunity to further connect the client with his own experience. But the responses provided by the Meta-model— "How do you know you are afraid of crowds?" or "What about crowds frightens you?" or "What stops you from being comfortable in crowds?"—serve to keep you with the client's experience, thus generating answers and new possibilities for growth from his own resources that even you may not have yet developed.

Finding those points at which you go inside to internal experience to understand the given communication and inserting the Meta-model questions there greatly enhances your effectiveness as a therapist and it facilitates integration of the Meta-model into automatic or unconscious behavior. One way to do this is by having a friend generate sentences that contain some *one* Meta-model violation. With each one, determine how your intuitions express themselves.

For example, with the statement "My feelings were hurt," if you make a picture, how did you know how her feelings were hurt, and by whom or what? Or, if you remember (whether visually, kinesthetically, or auditorily) a time when your own feelings were hurt, then you are "understanding" from your experience, not hers. As you become exquisitely aware of your own internal processes, you will learn those cues that signal you when you are going inside to make sense instead of staying in the present time-space coordinates. Once you have identified what your own signal is, you can utilize it by inserting the meta-model responses instead of your internalization. So, each time you hear that something is missing or doesn't make sense, you will know that a Meta-model response would be useful and appropriate.

The Meta-model is based on human intuitions. Therefore, by becoming explicitly aware of those intuitions, learning the Meta-model can be a quick and easy process. Those intuitions can be expressed in any representational system. If I say, for example, "The giraffe was chased," you have an intuition that something was left out. Perhaps your picture is incomplete or, if you represent kinesthetically, you don't know how fast the giraffe should be running. Neither of these is complete until you know the answer to: "Chased by what?" Regardless of how your intuitions express themselves, it is at that point that the Meta-model question is inserted in order to extract the fullest possible meaning from the communication.

To utilize these intuitions in teaching and learning the Meta-model distinctions, begin by: (1) generating sentences to the learner that contain one pattern of Meta-model violation; (2) ask the learner what his experience is; and (3) once you have determined how *the learner's* intuitions express themselves concerning this pattern, insert the appropriate Meta-model question as an integral portion of the expression of those same intuitions. So, if he has an incomplete picture, he asks for the rest of it. If he feels puzzled, insert the question that will put the pieces in place. If it doesn't sound right or it's "out of tune," insert the question that will make harmony of the discord. By varying the content of the statements containing Meta-model violations, the repetition necessary to integrate the Meta-model question with the intuition can remain stimulating. The intuitions will vary within a person for the various patterns. So, there may be a feeling for universal quantifiers, a picture for nominalizations, and a sound for cause and effect. Each person will have a unique set, but will fall into consistent generalizations. Once the patterns have been learned, there are exercises that can serve to further integrate them into everyday behavior.

Be sure to learn (or teach) the meta-model in the three categories outlined in this appendix: Gathering Information, Limits, and Semantic Ill-formedness. In this way, you (or the student) will have appropriately organized the meta-model for full integration into conscious and unconscious processes.

Notes

1. All quotations are from *The Structure of Magic I* by Richard Bandler and John Grinder; (Palo Alto, Ca; Science and Behavior Books, 1975)

Appendix II

Therapy Transcript

The following transcript of a more complete therapy session fully employs the techniques of anchoring and reframing. Hopefully, this presentation will provide you with a better understanding of how these techniques can be effectively used in the context of a therapeutic session.

S. Hello (hesitates in doorway, seems slightly disoriented).

Th. Hello, you must be Sheila. I'm happy to meet you. (Th. greets S. with extended hand, which she shakes. Th. then indicates chair for S. to sit in, to which S. responds first by eyeglance, then seating herself. Once seated, Th pulls up chair across from and close to S. so that it is within easy touching distance.)

Th. Just allow yourself to get comfortable, and we'll begin to learn from one another how I can assist you in making some changes which you desire.

S. Well, uhhh . . . I told you on the phone that my therapist referred me here. She said you do something different, something called neurolinguistic programming. (S. tonality high, nasal, flat; she looks up and left much of the time, her hands grip the arms of the chair.) I think she gave up on me (voice tone change, lower, softer; eyes upleft, then down and right).

Th. (Reaching over, takes S. by the hand gently.) Now, I don't even know yet what specifically you're here for, but I do know there is a strong possibility that you've misinterpreted your therapist's intention. A moment ago as you were talking of being referred here you were looking up and left. Was the picture you made of your therapist?

S. Huh?

Th. Look there again and tell me if you see her (indicates direction to look still holding one of S.'s hands).

S.   (Looks up and left again) Yes, but how did you know?

Th.   I'll explain in a moment, but first—I heard you say that you think she gave up on you, and I'm wondering if perhaps that wasn't the case at all. That perhaps it was actually quite difficult for her to refer you here, to suggest to you that someone else with a different set of tools could assist you when she could not. It seems to me that her referring you here might be an expression of care and concern from her that says she wants you to achieve those desired changes even without her. But, of course, you know her much better than I. So, go ahead, take a look at her again and *see* if this possibility *feels* any better.

S.   (Looks up and left, then down-right, sighs) You know, I think really you're right. She got frustrated with me, but now that I think about it, if she didn't care she wouldn't have bothered to send me here.

Th.   (Gently squeezes S.'s hand) This can be a new learning for you. I'll bet there have been other times when you assumed a negative message from what could and probably was a positive one. Is that true? (Th. looks up and right, which is a mirror for S.'s looking up and left.)

S.   (Looks up, left; nods) Why, yes.

Th.   (Squeezes hand gently) And you can begin now to be in touch with what the positive messages in those situations could have been? (Looks down and left, again mirror for S. looking down and right.) ANCHORING AND LEADING WITH ACCESSING CUES.

S.   Yes. Yes, I think I can. (Looks down and right, smiles.)

Th.   Good. Sometime this evening I want you to remember (looks up and right) at least three such times and then think of what the other messages (looks down and right), the possible positive ones, could have been, keeping this experience (squeezes hand gently) firmly in mind. Okay? (Smiles.)

S.   (Smiles) Okay. I'll do that.

Th.   (Releases hand, sits back slightly.) Now, tell me what is it that has brought you to therapy.

S.   (Responds immediately by slumping, looking sullen and dejected, eyes downcast.)

Th.   Whoa, whoa. (Reaches over, touches S. on thigh to get her attention back.) Hey, come back; no need to go there (Th. demonstrates S.'s posture, then smiles and leans forward). I've got it. Instead of telling me what brought you, tell me how you'll know when you don't need to come anymore.

S.   Well, ummm, I don't know (eyes up, left; down, right). It's just that, well, (eyes down left, fidgets) I'm frigid (this is said louder and somewhat explosively—then rapidly, with upturned palms) . . . and I've been in pre-orgasmic groups and read all the books and tried therapy, and still nothing . . . nothing . . . and now you.

Th.   (Allows a pause, then very directly) How do you know you are frigid?

S.   (Eyes up, left) Huh? What kind of question is that?

Th.   Now, I know that you have ways of determining what state of being you are in and what you are not. You have a way of knowing whether you are comfortable (pauses, S.'s eyes are down and right) or happy (pause) or curious, and so on. We human beings actually understand language by associating it with our experience. While still very young, you learned to connect some combination of pictures, feelings, sounds, smells with a word. Take the word "curious." How do you know when you are being curious?

S.   Well (eyes up-left, then down-left, over to right) I don't know; it's just a feeling (S. touches midline).

Th.   (Touches S.'s knee) The feeling of being curious is what you're aware of, but there was something else that helped trigger that feeling. You looked up and left, then down and over (Th. demonstrates). Remembering my question, look up there again, then down, and tell me what you're aware of.

S.   Oh! (surprised). I see the attic door in my house when I was a little girl (laughs). My mother was always telling me to stay out of it. That's where she kept our Christmas presents.

Th.   And you were very curious about those presents, weren't you? (Touches S.'s knee.)

S.   You bet.

Th.   Can you hear your mother's voice telling you to stay out of there?

S.   (Eyes down, left, smiles) Yes.

Th.   So you have ways (goes through analogue cues) to know when you are curious (P. touches S.'s knee—S nods). Now, how do you know you are frigid?

S.   Well . . . (eyes up left, then down left) because I don't have
orgasms.

Th.   What did you see up there?

S.   Oh, uhhh (eyes up, left again). I just see the group of women
in the women's group I was in. That's how all this began. I knew
sex wasn't real important to me, but it didn't seem to matter
much until that group. Since then, I just can't seem to get it off
my mind. It's like I'm a failure as a woman unless I can have
orgasms. I worked on that a lot in therapy and I know better, but
I still want to have orgasms.

Th.   If I understand you correctly, then you know you're frigid
since you don't have orgasms, and since you don't have orgasms
you know you're frigid?

S.   Yeah, that's right.

Th.   All right. How do you know you don't have orgasms?

S.   (Eyes up, left; then down, right; then up and right.) Because
I've never had anything like what the women in my group have
described or like what they say in the books.

Th.   (Eyes up, left to mirror up-right of S.) Tell me what you think
an orgasm would be like.

S.   They—the women and some of the books—said there were
plateaus and peaks and explosions of feelings . . . (while S.
talked, she continued to refer to her constructed images up and
right and to make the pictures with her hands). They said it was
different for each person, but I've never had anything like that
happen.

Th.   I see. In thinking back to our discussion about how we understand words—like how you know when you are curious—the
experience that you connect with the word "orgasm" is made up
of pictures; pictures you have constructed from descriptions
given you by other women and from books. My guess is that
since you don't experience these pictures as a result of having
sex, you've decided that you're not having orgasms.

S.   (Defensively) Are you saying I have?

Th.   No. What I am saying is that from what you've told me the
word "orgasm" is being understood in only one system: visual.
That's a bit like having the experience of swimming described
only in smells.

S.   I don't understand (eyes down, right).

Th.   You have been given descriptions in words, which you have translated into pictures. An orgasm is an entire experience, the most highly valued portion of which is usually feelings.

S.   But that's what I was talking about—feelings.

Th.   Can you feel a peak or a plateau? And probably your body would be unwilling to feel an explosion.

Let me explain: I can describe an orgasm as a rush of warm, exquisitely pleasurable sensations that emanate in waves to all parts of the body from the genitals, bringing relaxed, calm satisfaction in their wake. Now, if you have not had a kinesthetic experience with which to relate what I have said, you may instead translate it to a picture—say, to the sight of a stone being thrown into a quiet dark pond, and ripples moving outward in concentric circles to the edges of the pond until it is still again. That would be an excellent pictorial understanding of my description, but not what you could expect or hope to feel when you are orgasmic.

Th.   So I know even less about the whole thing that I thought I did?

Th.   Oh, I'm sure you know much more about this than you are conscious of knowing (touches S. on knee). And that part of you that is curious about having orgasms is probably as impatient as you were to find out about those Christmas presents in the attic. Is that true?

S.   (Eyes up, left) Yeah, I'm curious and impatient, and I don't like being left out. It's like other people are getting the goodies and I'm left out.

Th.   Excellent. You have a part that is curious and explores the world for new experience and wants to make sure you get to have those pleasurable experiences that it sees other people having. Ask that part if it can see anything to stop you from having orgasms.

S.   What? Ask what?

Th.   Ask inside if your curious part can see anything to stop you from having orgasms. Then look up and left since it expresses itself mostly in pictures for the answer.

S.   (Goes down and left; then up and left—head shakes no.) Nothing is there.

Th.   Good.

S.   Wait a minute! What's a part?

Th.   A part is a way of talking about aspects of you that express themselves in abilities to do or be something. As your ability to be curious, to be impatient to have a desired experience, we can call your "curious" part. Parts are originally developed from learnings derived from experience. We develop a cautious part from experiences like touching a hot stove, falling downstairs or off a bike. Such experiences produce pain, and so a cautious part —often visual in nature, looking out for danger—develops in order to protect us. All our parts are there for our benefit and are resources once we learn how to utilize them. That's what reframing is all about. It is a process by which you learn to contact your parts by being aware of your own internal processes (internal dialogue, visualizations, feelings, etc.) since this is how they express themselves to you, then learning what purpose they serve and how to utilize them to achieve desired changes as well as to lead a satisfying and pleasing life. Often, while parts are going about their business, they come into conflict with one another. Have you ever had a conflict between, say, your adventurous part and your cautious part?

S.   Oh, yeah. Usually I end up not doing anything and then feeling like I really missed out later.

Th.   With reframing, you would contact the cautious part and find out what reassurances or precautions it needed you to make in order to let you have an adventurous experience without its interference. After all, it serves a vital function of protecting you from danger. You can express your appreciation of it doing its task by satisfying its needs, and then you can go ahead and satisfy the adventurous part of you.

With that in mind, we can begin to explore the possibility of there being some part, which is unknown to you at this time, that prevents you from having orgasms.

S.   Well, if there is, I just want to get rid of it.

Th.   It would merely wait and come back, perhaps in a different form. Parts are born out of learnings from experiences. They are born to serve a purpose, and when an experience happens that seems to apply to that learning, they express themselves. Remember they are serving a purpose; each has a function and is doing the best it knows how to do. What you can do is change a part, educate it to do its job in a way more suited to your present desires and needs. But enough of this.

I want you to make a general declaration inside to all your

parts that you are now undertaking a new process of change, and that you will do your best to consider all of them and wish their cooperation on this venture. Okay?

S. Okay. (Bows head, closes eyes for a few moments, laughs.)

Th. What happened? Did you get a reply?

S. Well, I did like you said and I heard a round of applause.

Th. Excellent. Now announce to your parts that as a demonstration of this new process of change you are going to reorganize yourself in such a way as to be able, at appropriate times, to achieve orgasm. Go ahead—tell them.

S. (Closes eyes, tilts head up, left, then humphs and moves head down and right; smiles and opens eyes, looking pleased with herself.)

Th. (As S. looks down and right, P. touches her other knee.) It appears a lot went on in there.

S. Yeah, I told them what you said and first I got this voice that said "I'll believe it when I see it." And I got this sick feeling right here (indicates stomach/chest area) and another voice said "You'll believe it when it's felt, not seen."

Th. Marvelous. We know there's some parts in there already learning and willing to keep you headed in the right direction (down and right).

S. Huh?

Th. Now, I want you to begin to go through for yourself all the experiences you typically have when involved in intercourse. There is a series, a sequence of experiences, that leads to and follows an orgasm. Somewhere, your sequence is interrupted or leads to some experience other than an orgasm. We need to learn more about what happens to you. So, ask your parts, particularly your curious one, to go inside and, taking all the time you need, remember very vividly with exquisite detail a time when you were really aroused—you were eagerly anticipating the physical experience before you —and, beginning there, (reaches over, squeezes S.'s right knee as a distinct expression occurs) recall deeply how one feeling came to follow another.

S. (Sits back, breathes deeply, facial muscles relax, closes eyes. As she goes through this internal process, there is REM, color comes into her face, breathing rate increases for a while, rhythmic hand and foot movement though slight, lips swell slightly,

then at one point breathing stops, S. frowns slightly, body rigi-
difies. *All of this is subtle.*) All right, I did it. Now what?

Th.   What are you aware of most about what you just did?

S.   (Eyes down, right) That I have the same disgusted and disappointed feeling I have after I've really had sex.

Th.   I want to explain something about that awareness you are
experiencing right now. What you're aware of consciously is that
particular feeling. You may not be aware of your back against the
chair or the hum of the air conditioning or the smell of smoke
from cigarettes smoked here earlier today. At least you probably
weren't aware of them until I mentioned them and brought them
into consciousness. What we can consciously be aware of is
limited. Otherwise, we'd be overwhelmed. We select portions of
experience to be conscious of. I know that sexually you respond
to body smells, breathing rhythms, temperature changes,
sounds—all kinds of stimuli that you are not likely to be conscious of. Also, while you are responding to all the stimuli provided by the external world, particularly your partner—

S.   My husband.

Th.   —your husband, you are also responding to the portions of
experience you are generating internally: internal sounds, dialogue, imagery, feelings, etc. So, I'm going to ask you to do the
same thing over again, but this time a little differently. You can
have your curious part (P. squeezes S. on left knee as expression
comes up) and your aroused part (squeezes other knee; expression comes up) go with you, and they will pay special attention
to finding what stops you from achieving orgasm. Also, until this
learning has taken place, you can continue to review the events
of your sexual experience, becoming aware of all those aspects
you missed previously. The smells, sounds, special touches,
sights—all of them—perhaps attending to one, then another,
then adding them to one another.

S.   Sounds wonderful!

Th.   I agree. So, while you're doing that, your parts can do some
searching. Ask them if they are willing to participate.

S.   (Goes inside, looks up, nods head) Yes.

Th.   Good. Tell them they can allow one hand or the other, or
even both, to rise when they have made the appropriate discovery.

S.   (Goes inside) Okay. (S. goes through similar sequence of body changes as before, then goes through a second time. Just before frown is fully expressed, the right hand begins to rise.)

Th. (Reaches over, touches right hand) I understand. And when you have completed to your satisfaction the task, I want you to come all the way back here.

S. (Keeps eyes closed a while longer, then opens them, blinking.)

Th. Before you tell me what you've learned, take a couple of good breaths and give those parts a message of appreciation for what they've done.

S. (Smiles, breathes deeply.) Well, what I found out was that there are two things that stop me from having orgasms. One I knew was there, but I didn't know it kept me from having orgasms.

Th. Okay. Tell me about them in the natural sequence in which they occur.

S. (S.'s analogue assumes an "expression" previously seen in the middle of the series already exhibited. As she speaks, the sequence of "expressions" completes itself.) Well, just when I'm really getting into it, really beginning to enjoy it, I mean I can really feel the mounting sensations (stops, eyes down and left), this voice comes in and says, "Naughty, naughty. That's nasty and you're a bad girl."

Th. Whose voice is that?

S. (Down and left) Why, it's my mother's voice—she's spoiling it for me.

Th. Whoa, slow down. You said there were two. Continue telling me. What happens after your mother's voice?

S. Well, I never really heard her before, but after her comes my voice saying, "You did it again. You'll never make it now. No matter what, you can't do it."

Th. Okay. There are two parts that express themselves in internal dialogue. Ask inside if anything else gets in the way of your having orgasms besides these two parts.

S. (Goes inside) No, that's it.

Th. Now, this mother part you have . . . it tells you that what you're doing is naughty and nasty, is that right?

S. Yes.

Th. Can you hear her telling you that now?

S. Yes.

Th.   Good. Ask that part, call it a mother part if you like, what it's trying to do for you.

S.   (Goes inside) It says—you know, it's funny it really is my mother's voice (shrugs)—it says it's teaching me that sex is wrong and nasty.

P.   Ask it if it is trying to protect you from something it thinks is wrong and nasty.

Th.   (Goes inside) Yes, yes it is. But that's crazy. I don't think sex is bad or dirty. I know better than that.

P.   Yes, *you* do, but we're talking about a part that developed its learnings apparently from your mother. Let's check that out. Can you remember your mother telling you anything about sex?

S.   Oh yeah, she caught me and the boy next door playing doctor and she threw a fit.

Th.   Did she say anything about it being nasty and dirty?

S.   Yes.

Th.   As far as you know, does your mother think sex is nasty and dirty.

S.   She sure does.

P.   So, you have made many more learnings in this area than she had the opportunity to make. True?

S.   Yeah, I guess so.

Th.   Sometimes what mothers tell their daughters when they are young about sex is very different than what they say as their daughters become women. That is, they share teachings concerning sex that are appropriate as far as they are concerned for the stage of development their daughter is in.

S.   Not my mother. Sex got dirtier the older I got as far as she was concerned.

Th.   That's too bad. Now, I know that your mother was trying to protect you from experiences that for her were nasty and dirty. A part of you accepted her teachings, perhaps learning that your mother always had your best interests at heart and usually you did well as a child to heed her advice. So a part—your mother part—comes in with her warning each time you are sexually excited.

S.   Sure seems that way.

Th.   This part's growth was stunted concerning sex. Understandably so, if it received learnings from your mother and your mother's knowledge of sexual fulfillment is also limited.

S. I want my mother out of my sex life.

Th. Fine. My guess is, though, that as long as that part is concerned for your well-being—which you do appreciate don't you?

S. Yeah.

Th. —and it thinks sex is bad for you, it will continue to interfere in unpleasant ways about your reaching a state of sexual fulfillment. Ask inside if this is true.

S. (Does so) Yes. So what now?

Th. Ask this part what it needs in order to stay out of this portion of your life, comfortably.

S. (Asks inside) It says, to know I'll be okay.

Th. Good. Ask it if it was reassured that sexual fulfillment was good for you, and even necessary for you to achieve the development of your full potential as a person as well as a woman, would it stay out of this area of your life?

S. My mother would never believe it.

Th. But this is a part of you—not your mother. It's a part that is based on learnings from your mother, but it is still a part of you and has access to all those learnings you have made since you were a little girl. So ask her.

S. Okay (goes inside). It says yes, but how?

Th. Do you have children?

S. No, but I hope to.

Th. Now, even though this part has your mother's voice, it was created when you were young and it has not grown up with you. Even though you don't have children now, if you did—if you had a daughter whom you wanted to teach about the wonders of womanhood and sexuality, a daughter whom you wanted to get even more out of her sexual experiences than you have—there would be much to say to her. True?

S. Yes. I'd sure do it differently than my mother.

Th. Excellent. And now in your mind's eye, take that part of you by the hand. Walk through life's highway with her and teach her in a gentle and reassuring way about what it means to be a woman. Surprise and delight her with all you know, giving her what she needs to be an adequate mother part for you—including finding a place in your life where she will be useful.

S. Okay.

Th. Good. Just close your eyes, take all the time you need, and you can enjoy this process of teaching your mother part about being a woman, can you not? That's right. And when you've completed this journey to your complete satisfaction, you can come back but no sooner than *all* parts are satisfied that the important learnings of human sexuality have been accomplished.

S.   (Settles back, spends about 12 minutes sitting quietly, eyes closed, breathing regularly, sometimes deeply. Comes back, blinks, opens eyes, sits up) Okay (smiles, looks pleased, relaxed).

Th.   Well, you look pleased.

S.   Oh, I am.

Th.   And in what area of your life have you found a place for your mother?

S.   In the kitchen. She can really cook and she is going to help me in the kitchen. We're going to do some great things.

Th.   And is she content to stay out of the bedroom?

S.   Oh, yes. Yes. You know, I didn't know I knew all those things I taught her.

Th.   I believe you. Sometimes teaching can be the best way to learn.

S.   Huh.

Th.   Now, as I recall, there was another voice that interfered with the natural order of things. Right?

S.   Oh, yeah. I forgot about that. Wow! I feel so good about what you just did.

Th.   Hey, *you* did it, not me. Remember that. (Copies S.'s analogue behavior from before.) That other voice . . . it said, "Uh-oh, you blew it, you'll never make it now." Right?

S.   Yeah, I can hear it now. It's my voice.

Th.   Ask that part if it wants you to have an orgasm.

S.   (Does so) Yes, it says yes.

Th.   Good. Ask it if it feels this will be easier now that mother is gone.

S.   (Does so) Yeah (some hesitation).

Th.   But it's not really sure how.

S.   Huh-uh (shakes head no).

Th.   Ask it to listen carefully while I suggest a special strategy for it to use to enhance your sexual experience. If it agrees that this is a good strategy and will use it, it can tell you by giving you a warm, good, satisfied feeling through here (indicating lower abdominal and pelvic area). Okay?

S. Yes.

Th. I'm glad you agree, but ask inside just to make sure.

S. (Does so) Yeah. (Nods, eyes down and right.) I already feel kind of excited.

Th. Somehow this part is paying exquisite attention to your sexual experience and tells you when it doesn't think you are going to achieve an orgasm. Presently, it serves to distract you from the very stimulus that will increase your pleasure. I suggest to this part that it use its skills to enhance your experience and even guide you to an orgasm.

S. How?

Th. By using that internal dialogue to describe to you all the aspects of your experience. To pace you. To describe where your body is touching his, to describe sensuously to you the smells, breathing patterns, rhythms of movement, always using positive terms, guiding you, making sure you stay immersed in the experience you're involved in. Constantly enhancing your experience. Finding what pleases you more and taking you there. In essence, utilizing that part as a primary resource, making sure it is closely associated with your ability to be aroused.

S. It's happening. I almost don't believe it, but it's telling me "yes" just like you said.

Th. Great. Now, just to make sure, go back, all the way back, and allow it to escort you through an imaginary sexual experience using the strategies I have suggested.

S. (Goes inside.)

Th. Let it take you all the way through.

S. (Appropriate analogue for described task.) God, that's great! I'm ready!

Th. For?

S. For my new sex life. My husband is going to really be surprised.

Th. Be sure to give him some credit for your new experiences. After all, he is going to play an important part.

S. Of course (smiling).

Th. Ask inside if there is anything left undone in this matter.

S. (Does so) No, everything is great. I feel terrific!

Th. Thinking back for a moment, remember what it was like to discover parts of yourself so you can find them when you need

to. You often need to make contact with them in order to increase your choices with them.

S.   Yeah, I think I can do that.

Th.   I want to share with you, now, some ways that have made
your parts available to me to communicate with. We call them
anchors. You may have noticed that I have touched you frequently.

S.   Yeah, I thought it a little strange at first, but it was nice.

Th.   Thank you, I like making contact. But, besides that, they
were also ways for me to "call" parts of you out. Pay attention
to your experience while I demonstrate. (Fires off anchors one
at a time.)

S.   That is incredible. I really felt myself change.

Th.   Now you do it for yourself and learn how they can work for
you.

S.   It does, but not as much as when you do it.

P.   It will. You just have to learn what you're going for. Whenever
you wish to contact your curious part that is also impatient for
you to have the richest, fullest life possible, just squeeze your left
knee gently and remember the picture of that attic door. That
curious feeling will let you know that part is accessing itself to
you. Go ahead, try it now.

S.   You're right.

Th.   Of course. Also, if you wish, you can let your husband in on
a secret. If he would like to arouse you in a subtle and pleasant
way, he can merely give a gentle squeeze to your right knee. Like
this (squeezes right knee).

S.   (Color comes to face, smiles) What have you done to me?

Th.   That particular touch has become associated for you with the
experience of being aroused . . . of anticipating a more full
physical contact. We call them anchors. They become tied to
particular experiences. Also, now that you know about it, you
can respond even more, allowing your conscious awareness to
join your unconscious response. Do you have any questions?

S.   Probably, but not right now.

Th.   Well, take a few moments and review the process we have
gone through so you can do it on your own, remembering how
you made contact with parts, learned from them and about them
in a way that would allow you to achieve those desired changes.

S.   (Closes eyes, is quiet for several minutes.) Okay.

Th.   Good. I'd like you to come back in two weeks and we'll review what changes have taken place and you can pick some other change you would like to make. Then you can use this process with me available, for trouble shooting, in order to make sure you can effect change and gain new choices on your own. Okay?

S.   Sure, and thanks. Thanks a lot.

SELECTED BIBLIOGRAPHY

Ard, B., and Ard, C. *Handbook of Marriage Counseling.* Palo Alto, CA: Science and Behavior Books, 1973.

Bandler, R., and Grinder, J. *The Structure of Magic, Volume I.* Palo Alto, CA: Science and Behavior Books, 1975.

————. *The Structure of Magic, Volume II.* Palo Alto, CA: Science and Behavior Books, 1976.

————. *Patterns of the Hypnotic Techniques of Milton H. Erickson, M.D., Volume I.* Cupertino, CA: Meta Publications, 1976.

————. *Patterns of the Hypnotic Techniques of Milton H. Erickson, M.D., Volume III.* Cupertino, CA: Meta Publications, forthcoming.

Bandler, R.; Grinder, J.; and DeLozier, J. *Patterns of the Hypnotic Techniques of Milton H. Erickson, M.D., Volume II.* Cupertino, CA: Meta Publications, 1977.

Bandler, R.; Grinder, J.; Satir, V. *Changing with Families.* Palo Alto, CA: Science and Behavior Books, 1976.

Belliveau, F., and Richter, L. *Understanding Human Sexual Inadequacy.* New York: Little, Brown and Co., 1970.

Berne, E. *Sex in Human Loving.* New York: Simon & Schuster, 1970.

Ellis, A. *The Art and Science of Love.* New York: Lyle Stewart, 1960.

————. *The Sensuous Person.* New York: The New American Library, 1974.

————. *Sex Without Guilt.* New York: Lyle Stewart, 1958.

Fried, E. *On Love and Sexuality.* New York: Grune & Stratton, 1960.

Jaynes, J. *The Origin of Consciousness in the Breakdown of of the Bicameral Mind.* New York: Houghton Mifflin, 1976.

Laing, R. D. *The Politics of the Family.* New York: Random House (Vintage Press), 1969.

Marshall, D., and Suggs, R. *Human Sexual Behavior.* The Institute for Sex Research, 1972.

Masters, W., and Johnson, V. *Human Sexual Inadequacy.* New York: Little, Brown and Co., 1970.

―――. *Human Sexual Response.* New York: Little, Brown and Co., 1966.

―――. *The Pleasure Bond.* New York: Little, Brown and Co., 1975.

Perls, F. *The Gestalt Approach and Eye Witness to Therapy.* Palo Alto, CA: Science and Behavior Books, 1973.

Slater, P. *Footholds.* Canada: Clark Irwin Co., 1968.

Watzlawick, Weakland, and Fisch. *Change.* New York: W. W. Norton Co., 1974.